SCIENCE AND THE CHRISTIAN FAITH

A Guide for the Perplexed

▪▪ Foundations series

Testifying to the faith and creativity of the Orthodox Christian
Church, the Foundations series draws upon the riches of its
tradition to address the modern world. These survey texts are
suitable both for preliminary inquiry and deeper investigation,
in the classroom and for personal study.

Peter C. Bouteneff

Series Editor

BOOK 8 OF THE FOUNDATIONS SERIES

Science and the Christian Faith

A GUIDE FOR THE PERPLEXED

CHRISTOPHER C. KNIGHT

ST VLADIMIR'S SEMINARY PRESS
YONKERS, NEW YORK
2020

Library of Congress Cataloging-in-Publication Data

[Names: Knight, Christopher C., 1952– author.
Title: Science and the Christian faith : a guide for the perplexed /
 Christopher C. Knight.
Description: Yonkers, New York : St Vladimir's Seminary Press, 2020. |
 Series: Foundations series, 1556-9837 ; book 8 | Summary: "In Science
 and the Orthodox Faith Fr Christopher C. Knight addresses the question
 of the relationship between science and Christian faith from the
 perspective of the Orthodox Church. This contributes a unique voice to
 the field, drawing upon the tradition of the Orthodox Church, both
 ancient and modern"-- Provided by publisher.
Identifiers: LCCN 2020038189 (print) | LCCN 2020038190 (ebook) | ISBN
 9780881416718 (paperback) | ISBN 9780881416725 (kindle edition)
Subjects: LCSH: Religion and science. | Orthodox Eastern Church--Doctrines.
Classification: LCC BL240.3 .K589 2020 (print) | LCC BL240.3 (ebook) |
 DDC 261.5/5--dc23
LC record available at https://lccn.loc.gov/2020038189
LC ebook record available at https://lccn.loc.gov/2020038190

The publication of this book has been made possible by the
Science and Orthodoxy around the World (SOW) project,
which is funded by the Templeton World Charity Foundation Inc.
The contents reflect the author's own opinions, however, and do not
necessarily reflect those of either the project or the Foundation.

ST VLADIMIR'S SEMINARY PRESS
575 Scarsdale Road
Yonkers, New York 10707
914-961-8313
www.svspress.com

ISSN 1556-9837
ISBN 978-088141-671-8 (print)
ISBN 978-088141-672-5 (digital)

PRINTED IN THE UNITED STATES OF AMERICA

*This book is dedicated to the parishioners
and clergy—living and departed—of the
Parish of the Holy Transfiguration, Walsingham,
England, in which I have the privilege
of serving as parish priest.*

CONTENTS

FOREWORD

Recent decades have seen no shortage of books and commentary about "science and religion." Within these, if we're lucky, we might find some subtle and nuanced thinking, helping us to learn both about faith and about science. We are at least shown that it is worth thinking on these things.

Yet there is a persistence of crude arguments, possibly because these attract more attention and sell more copies. Some scientists will argue that religion is a fantasy world antithetical to scientific reality. Some "religious" voices claim that science is all theories, many of them specious, and that we answer to a higher authority: the Bible—which can only be read as a literal account of astronomy, geology, zoology, and history. There is no shortage of self-righteousness on either side. The opposition is painted either as simple reason vs. mad fervor, or as spiritual wisdom vs. secular faithlessness.

If you are frustrated by both sides of such arguments, this book is for you.

Because, if I am correct, you are looking for a book written by someone versed in both Christian teaching and life as well as in the methods and realities of scientific inquiry. You want the author to be an inquisitive person who is unafraid of ideas, who will give them due consideration. You want someone who can write out of the lived experience of science and of a practiced, believed faith. You have that author here, and this book reflects all those desired (and relatively rare) characteristics.

When such a book is written by a believing and practicing Christian, how much does it matter whether the author is a Protestant, a Catholic, an Orthodox? On some levels it hardly matters at all; the author's basic faith, knowledge, lived experience, and curiosity may be more consequential. Yet on other levels, Christian confession matters a great deal. For example, what *sources* are most meaningful to the Christian author's arguments? One hopes that the Bible would be held in common as an authoritative voice. For an Orthodox author, however, the importance of early Christian witness is also paramount. The "Fathers" of the Church (who also include Mothers) are those persons entrusted with how to read and understand the Bible. Because, as one of these trusted witnesses said himself, back in the fourth century, "Scripture is not in the reading but in the understanding."[1] Scripture is not a self-interpreting text.

Recourse to these ancient authorities and other theological and liturgical sources is one of the useful and distinguishing features of this book. We learn about how they read their Bible and their world, and how each informs the other. You may ask, "When a fourth-century bishop writes on matters of science and faith, how is it relevant to us moderns and post-moderns?" You may also rightly point out that what "science" even meant in the late-ancient Near East is completely different from what we mean by the word today. While we ought to be wary of anachronism—asking modern questions of premodern texts—there are lessons from the past that we can justly apply today, even with all our intellectual and technological advances. Some examples follow.

---

[1]Hilary of Poitiers, *Ad Constantium Aug. Bk. 2.9.* Hilary is perhaps echoing the words of the Ethiopian who, while reading from Isaiah, asks the apostle Philip, "How can I understand, unless someone guides me?" (Acts 8.31).

One of the transformative insights we gain from this study is that our first-millenium forebears were not "biblical literalists," in the sense of reading the Bible solely in a literal way. Yes, they believed that the Bible records things that happened (in the form of stories, histories, prayers, parables, etc.), but also that different books in the bible functioned in different ways. (The word for "the Bible" in Greek is plural—*ta biblia*—the *books*.) Different books, and even different passages within the same books, were read in quite different ways. Even some of the very same passages were read *both* historically and allegorically. In the case of some—among them the early chapters of Genesis—the allegorical and moral meanings took precedence. And the readings that always took pride of place were the *Christological* (or "typological"), where Adam was seen in relation to Christ, Eve in relation to Mary. "The beginning" in which the world was created was understood as Christ—"the alpha and omega; the beginning and the end" (Rev 22.13). These insights are fascinating enough on their own, but then we imagine what they imply for our own reading of Genesis, with the additional data that the universe is probably about fourteen billion years old. And the Bible reveals that this very cosmos is created by Christ and transformed in him.

Fr Christopher Knight, a trained astrophysicist and ordained Orthodox theologian, is well positioned to ask the right questions, redirect misleading questions, and take us on a journey towards their exploration and resolution. He begins appropriately with attention to fundamental questions about the relationship of science and faith. He gives insight into both sides—crucially distinguishing science from scien*tism*, and faith from sheer literalism. That essential nuance is one key to liberating us from the logjam of pointless polemics between positions that have no room for each other, not to mention no personal charity, and no intellectual curiosity—like those between the "New Atheists" and Biblical literalists.

Fr Christopher devotes considerable attention to questions about the origins and age of the universe and the creation of the human person. But he discusses many other questions that are not as headline-making but are nonetheless consequential. As one example, he justly devotes an entire chapter to the question of "natural theology," where he probes the assets and liabilities of a close reading of Romans 1.20. He also goes further into the term "nature" itself, which admits multiple meanings, whether it is referring to the created cosmos, or to the humanity and divinity, respectively, of Jesus Christ. In so doing, he is demonstrating an entire approach to reading Scripture and the Fathers such that we are not parroting them or proof-texting, but getting at what they really meant to tell us.

Another example of the author's approach is his chapter on "Naturalism and the Miraculous." Like so much of this book, this chapter will invite us to think, and think anew, on what we mean by words like "natural," "supernatural" and—if this one is even in our vocabulary — "subnatural." Fr Christopher never dismisses scientific arguments ("You just have to have faith!"), but he does reveal some of their limitations, and the problems that arise when they are applied to theological questions. In this way, this book respects science in a way that gives space for the operation of what people of faith accept as absolute reality.

Furthermore, the author is unafraid to say that people of faith can gain a great deal from science, even in our theological think-ing. A prime example is in this book's chapters on the human mind. Science, Fr Christopher notes, helps us redress the residual body/soul dualism we can find in some Christian reflection, which distorts the Christian (and biblical) holistic understanding of the human person. Of course, science and faith can often talk at cross purposes in such areas too. I recall seeing a neuroscientist on a talk show, who said, "Now that we've mapped the human brain, I guess that's proof that there is no such thing as a soul!" Here again, Fr Christopher does not shy away from talking about brain scans and what they do and do not tell us about body, soul, and mind. In all, he concludes that science can help us in reappropriating the ancient Christian teaching on the human person, on life, death, and resurrection.

I am grateful for this book, for making me think and think anew on questions I thought I had resolved, and consider questions that I had not before. I believe it will become an indispensable resource to the Christian apologist, as well as to those interested in how Orthodox Christians frame the science/faith encounter. Finally, the inviting and learned quality of the writing makes this a book both to learn from and enjoy.

Peter Bouteneff
Feast of the Elevation of the Cross
2020

INTRODUCTION

For members of the Orthodox Church, the sciences of our time can seem to present a number of awkward and even faith-threatening questions. If, for example, we accept that the cosmos operates according to laws of nature, does this mean that our belief in the miraculous is questionable? If we accept the scientific evidence for the physical basis for much of the mental activity that has traditionally been associated with the soul, must we abandon our belief in eternal life? If we accept what the scientists say about our universe's history, does this mean that we must abandon what the Scriptures seem to say about that history and what the Fathers of the Church often believed?

In the face of questions of this kind, some argue that we must make a choice between current scientific theory and our Orthodox faith. We can't assert the validity of one, they say, without denying the validity of the other. But there are others among us who question this view, and I am one of them. In this book I shall explain why. I shall argue that although the questions raised by current scientific theories are far from negligible for those of us who hold the Orthodox faith, we do not need to answer those questions by rejecting science.

In my own adoption of this position, my personal history is a factor. Although I am now a priest of the Orthodox Church, in my childhood and early adulthood I was fascinated by science. Because of this, I initially pursued a scientific path in my education, being trained to Ph.D. level in astrophysics before recognizing that theology had an even greater fascination for me. This recognition led me to abandon my potential scientific career and to take a degree in Christian theology. Nevertheless, even after this change of direction, science did not cease to interest me, and the question of whether science and theology were in conflict was inevitably one that I had to face at a personal level. This led me to a careful study of their relationship and eventually to accept invitations to teach about that relationship and to write about it. This in turn led me to work, for the ten years immediately prior to my retirement, as the Executive Secretary of the International Society for Science and Religion. (The Fellows of this Society—of whom I am one—are elected on the basis of significant academic publications on the relationship of science to religious faith.)

In my teaching and writing, what I have always stressed is that it is not necessary for those of us who are Christians to reject the naturalistic methodological assumptions at the heart of the scientific project. What is necessary, I have insisted, is to understand naturalism at a deeper level than the average scientist does, not denying the validity of science but seeing it from the perspective of the religious believer. The issue, I have argued, is not one of having to choose between science and faith, but one of interpreting scientific methods and theories from an adequate philosophical and theological perspective. When this is done, I have urged, no conflict arises and in fact our theology is enriched.

In two previous books,[1] aimed mainly at academic audiences, I have in various ways presented my views about this consonance between science and Christian theology. While the second of these volumes put more stress on Orthodox perspectives, both of these volumes took Western Christian thinking about the relationship

---

[1]These are: *Wrestling With the Divine: Religion, Science, and Revelation* (Minneapolis: Fortress, 2001), and *The God of Nature: Incarnation and Contemporary Science* (Minneapolis: Fortress, 2007).

between science and theology as their starting point. Because they related to a debate that had taken place largely among Western Christians, they also had a Western audience in mind. The present book, by contrast, is aimed specifically at an Orthodox audience and focuses on the kinds of questions that I find are often asked in Orthodox circles.

It is different from those earlier books in another way, too. It is aimed, not primarily at academics, but at the ordinary, intelligent believer whose formal education may have included neither science nor theology at an advanced level. For this reason, it does not attempt a comprehensive survey of the work of others engaged in what is sometimes called the science-theology dialogue, and although it uses footnotes to indicate the sources of quotations and to give indications of possible further reading, it does not provide the usual academic apparatus of exhaustive references.

One of the ways that I shall address the issues often raised by ordinary Orthodox believers is to stress that science and theology focus on different kinds of questions. Science, I shall emphasize, is limited to answering what we might call "how" questions. It attempts to explain the *mechanisms* by which our cosmos operates and has developed. Theology, I shall suggest, is very different. It focuses on what we might call "why" questions, and our attempt to answer these "why" questions can lead us, in combination with faith, to understanding the cosmos's *purpose*. This distinction between "how" and "why" questions does not, I shall suggest, mean that the two kinds of questions never interact, as some have supposed. Rather, it means that scientists inevitably reach a point at which their discipline can take them no further. They need to recognize that there are legitimate questions to which science can give no answers.

Many scientists do in fact recognize this. Some of these, because they are unable to find persuasive answers to their "why" questions, have become *agnostics*. By adopting this term to identify themselves, they acknowledge that they simply "don't know" whether or not religious notions have any legitimacy. By contrast, those among them who are religious believers are confident that, over and above the scientific framework that allows them to explore "how" questions, there also exists a legitimate and complementary theological framework through which their "why" questions can be explored.

This situation is complicated, however, by a second group of non-believing scientists, who often make enough noise to make them seem the majority (though they are probably not). These have managed to convince themselves that God's non-existence can be definitely known, so that they have gone beyond simple agnosticism and proclaim the necessity of *atheism*.

These atheists often insist that the "why" questions that humans ask are not legitimate questions at all. In their view, only the scientific methodology can provide legitimate knowledge. This view is often referred to as *scientism,* and this scientism needs to be carefully distinguished from science itself. As the existence of religiously-inclined scientists indicates, scientism is not an intrinsic part of the pursuit of understanding the cosmos through the methods of the sciences. It represents a philosophical opinion, which for reasons that we shall examine has long been abandoned by most academic philosophers.

A kind of scientism was, admittedly, popular in the community of philosophers around the middle of the twentieth century, in the form that was known as *logical positivism*, but the kind of scientism now often proclaimed by atheistic scientists manifests little of the philosophical sophistication of that now-abandoned understanding. As philosophers of the present time have often pointed out, atheistic scientists who try to defend the tenets of scientism often find themselves, not just upholding a redundant philosophical position, but failing to do so in a coherent or well-informed way. The biologist Richard Dawkins, for example, has been criticized in this respect by a fellow-atheist, the philosopher Michael Ruse, who has famously said that Dawkins is the kind of atheist who makes him ashamed to be an atheist.[2]

Recognition that much current atheism is based on incoherent arguments does not, however, absolve us from the need to address the questions that some in our Orthodox community believe we face. For example, we clearly need to to find a coherent way of speaking about how miraculous events relate to a cosmos characterized by obedience to "laws of nature." We need also to ask whether speaking about the soul and about eternal life can ever be consistent with our scientific understanding of mental processes. We need, in addition, to ask serious questions about the way in which the picture of creation provided by the Scriptures and the works of the Church Fathers can seem at odds with the current scientific consensus.

The first of these issues, I shall suggest, is often approached in the wrong way. The question of how miracles are to be understood becomes a very different one than that usually assumed if we abandon the notions of the "supernatural" that are now prevalent in discussions about miracles. These notions—although common among Orthodox—have in fact arisen, as we shall see, from a tendency to separate grace and nature that arose in Western Christian theology, and this separation is not to be found in mainstream Orthodox thinking.

In the Eastern patristic tradition, I shall argue, events that are *above nature* are seen as arising, not from some process in which God is seen as a kind of outside agent who has no continuous

[2]*http://www.beliefnet.com/columnists/scienceandthesacred/2009/08/ why-i-think-the-new-atheists-are-a-bloody-disaster.html*. For Ruse's own more balanced approach, see Michael Ruse, *Atheism: What Everyone Needs to Know* (Oxford: Oxford University Press, 2015).

presence in his creation. Instead, I shall stress, God is seen as intimately connected to the cosmos, and his action is always from within that cosmos. In this understanding, I shall urge, miraculous events represent, not the "supernatural" action of of an outside agent, but an anticipation of the character of the "world to come." The state that these events unveil is *above nature* only in the sense that it is above the *subnatural* state in which, because of the fall, we now find ourselves. Miracles represent the *true nature* of the world intended by God in his creation of it.

The second of these issues—that which relates to the soul— may be seen in a new light, I shall suggest, if we take a sufficiently critical view of the kind of dualism in which the body and mind are viewed as distinct entities in some kind of loose association. We need to recognize that to understand the soul in these terms— as some philosophers did in both the ancient and early modern periods—is entirely wrong from an Orthodox perspective. The Orthodox position, as we shall see, has always been that body and mind are components of a unified being. It is partly because of this that Orthodox have always conceived eternal life, not in terms of the survival of a disembodied soul, but in terms of a resurrection body. In the light of this understanding, scientific insights can actually be helpful to us provided that they are inter-preted correctly.

What I shall argue in relation the third of these issues—the apparent incompatibilities between science's picture of the history of the cosmos and the biblical and patristic witness—is that these incompatibilities arise only when that witness is read at a superfi-cial level. The Fathers themselves, as I shall indicate, often under-stood Scripture at a deeper level than this surface one, and the way in which they themselves used the science and philosophy of their time points us towards both a deeper reading of their own works and a model on which we should base our own response to the sciences. When we undertake this deeper reading and adopt this model, the kind of fundamentalism that effectively says "this is the science that the Fathers believed and we must therefore believe the same" becomes something that we must clearly reject.

Part of the point here is that loyalty to our faith, while rightly involving a sense of the centrality of the Orthodox Tradition, needs to be based on a proper understanding of what the term *Tradition* means. In the English language, we Orthodox usually write this word with a capital T in order to indicate our belief in the inspiration of the Church, especially in the patristic age in which our doctrinal framework was systematized. This inspiration enabled our forebears to sift truly inspired and authoritative understandings from errors or mere opinions. Even so, Orthodoxy has always acknowledged that Tradition depends on consensus, and that not everything written by a particular patristic author is to be seen as part of Tradition. There is, as Metropolitan Kallistos of Diokleia has rightly observed, always a need to distinguish "Patristic wheat . . . from Patristic chaff."[3] This chaff, as we shall see, includes the inaccuracies of the somewhat primitive science that the Fathers sometimes used to illustrate their theological understanding.

It should perhaps be noted, before we begin to look at these arguments in detail, that some readers may be liable, in different ways, to misread them. The need to take these potential misunderstandings into account explains why—particularly towards the end of the book—there is a certain amount of repetition of the main components of those arguments. This repetition is based on the old advice to preachers that, if their message is to be effectively communicated, they should "say what they're going to say; then say it; then say what they've just said." I trust that those who do

---

[3]Timothy Ware, *The Orthodox Church* (Harmondsworth: Penguin, 1957), 212.

not need this kind of reinforcement will forgive the assumption that at least some of my readers might.

My belief and my prayer is that the readers of this book will find nothing in what I write that is contrary to the Orthodox Tradition, but will in fact discover in it a framework within which to develop a fuller and deeper understanding of that Tradition. They will, I trust, come to see that the sciences of our time provide us with an opportunity, not only to deepen our theological understanding, but also to see in new ways how, as the psalmist puts it, "the heavens declare the glory of the Lord."

chapter one

SCIENCE AND
THEOLOGICAL
INTERPRETATION

S ome Orthodox Christians have argued that the current scientific account of the history of the cosmos needs to be challenged, yet they often fail to recognize fully that this scientific account is underpinned by overwhelming evidence. Science, as we shall see, progresses through the way in which predictions that have been made by scientific theories have been confirmed by subsequent experiment or observation. What constitutes well-established scientific theory is that which has been strengthened by such predictive success.

Moreover, it is often the case that independent aspects of this evidence converge on the solution that now represents the accepted scientific account. For example, our scientific understanding of the age of the cosmos arises primarily from observations of the universe's expansion, which led to the Big Bang understanding of the universe's beginning. This understanding was developed originally because of observations of Doppler-effect changes in the observed wavelengths of electromagnetic radiation from distant galaxies. The theory was later reinforced by its correct prediction of the relative abundances of the two most common elements in the universe, hydrogen and helium, and—later still—by observation of the cosmic microwave background predicted by the theory. Refinement of our understanding of this Big Bang scenario still goes on, but this convergence of independent streams of evidence means that it is highly unlikely that this understanding will ever be overturned in any fundamental way.

In a comparable way, our scientific picture of evolution through natural selection arose originally from Charles Darwin's observations of differences between closely related species and subspecies. It was later reinforced and refined, however, both by fossil evidence and by genetic insights quite unknown to Darwin himself. These genetic insights were themselves later underpinned by biochemical insights that arose through the work that followed the discovery of the structure of DNA, and by technical advances that now enable us to look in detail at the genetic makeup of all living things. Once again, although this Neo-Darwinian scenario is still being refined, it seems highly unlikely that it will ever be overturned in any fundamental way. (The failure of attempts to replace Neo-Darwinism through the concept of "intelligent design" is something that we shall look at presently.) Thus, although at the level of detail there are still legitimate scientific arguments to be pursued, the scientific consensus about how the universe came to have its present character cannot convincingly be challenged as a whole.

Here, we need to understand the misleading nature of the critique of current scientific understanding that is sometimes made by saying that the Big Bang and evolutionary theories are "just theories." To some this may initially seem plausible because, in common usage, the term *theory* is often used to indicate an idea that is little more than a hunch that something might be true. In scientific usage, however, such a hunch might be referred to as a tentative hypothesis, though even the term *hypothesis* usually refers to something that already has a significant degree of support from good evidence. To speak about a well-established scientific theory as "just a theory" is to fail to take seriously its well-established nature. Even though, as we shall see presently, no scientific theory can ever be said to have been absolutely verified, there are certain theories that possess a considerable degree of robustness, and this robustness needs to be acknowledged.[1]

A quite different factor also needs to be considered by those Christians who reject modern scientific understandings. This is the issue of how the Christian faith is to be defended in the modern world. The robustness of the present scientific consensus means that those Christians who insist that their faith is incompatible with that consensus often present an enormous barrier to those who are scientifically literate but who might be willing to explore the Christian view of the world. In effect, these potential converts are told by the anti-science propagandists that they can only become Christians by committing intellectual suicide. Those of us who argue that Christianity is consonant with modern science are, by contrast, doing something comparable to what the Christian

[1]Even if current theories are eventually replaced, the history of science indicates that they will still very probably be seen as at least approximately true, in the sense that they will continue to provide understanding over a wide range of circumstances. The physicist of the present day, for example, knows that the dynamical theories of Isaac Newton, developed in the seventeenth century, are "wrong" in a way that their replacement—the twentieth century theories of Albert Einstein—have yet to be demonstrated as wrong. Nevertheless, for most purposes—essentially those in which no velocities comparable to that of light are involved—Newton's equations can still be used to get results that exhibit a high degree of accuracy. They are certainly "wrong" in a sense that we can understand, since they make assumptions about the absoluteness of space and time that we know to be mistaken, not only theoretically but also experimentally. Nevertheless, the Newtonian equations, despite their inadequacies, can still be seen to be "approximately true" over a wide range of circumstances in that they make correct predictions, and—because they are easier to use than relativistic equations—they are in practice still used by physicists in those circumstances.

apologists of the second and third centuries were doing in relation to the Hellenic science and philosophy of their time.

Although these early apologists—people like St Justin Martyr and St Clement of Alexandria—developed ideas that later became the basis for much of the church's doctrinal articulation of the Christian faith, in their own time these defenders of the faith were not, first and foremost, attempting to formulate doctrine. Rather, they were trying to convince their educated contemporaries that acceptance of the Christian faith did not require the wholesale abandonment of what were held at the time to be valid scientific and philosophical insights. It is precisely this kind of apologetic task that has been taken up once again in our own day by those who proclaim that it is possible to appreciate all that science tells us and at the same time to be Christian. We Orthodox need, in my judgment, to affirm the motivation of these present-day apologists, even if—as we shall see—we also need to be vigilant to ensure that nothing that is central to our faith is abandoned or diluted in the process of developing apologetic arguments of this kind.

What, then, is the scientific consensus that the apologists of the present day are trying to take into account in their attempt to express the Christian faith for our own time? Briefly, the picture is as follows. Our universe seems to operate in a consistent manner through what we can call "laws of nature." These, at the most basic level, can be expressed in mathematical form and have proved to be explorable through what we now think of as a scientific methodology.

Observation and experiment, coupled with our understanding of these laws, allow us to affirm with a high degree of confidence that the universe had its beginning more than 13 billion years ago.[2] After the *Big Bang* that constituted this beginning, clouds

---

[2]The question of what was going on before this beginning is, for scientists, a meaningless one, just as it was for those Fathers of the Church who

of hydrogen and helium eventually formed, and the first stars developed from these clouds through gravitational collapse. In the cores of the more massive of these stars, new chemical elements such as carbon—which is necessary for life—were synthesized through nuclear fusion. In the death throes of these first stars, these new elements were spread into the interstellar medium. New generations of stars were born from this enriched medium, and they too, as they died, added to the store of heavier elements that were needed if complex chemical compounds—and ultimately we ourselves—were to be possible.

Some four and a half billion years ago, the star that we know as the Sun came into being. Like other stars in the early stages of their formation, it had around it a disk of gas, in which were embedded particles of dust and ice formed from the core materials of stars that had already died. As with other newly forming stars, some of this disk material around the newborn Sun eventually coalesced into planets. One of these planets was our Earth, whose mass, orbital distance, and other attributes were such that it developed conditions in which ever more complex carbon-based molecules could form and eventually become self-replicating. Life had begun, and among the creatures that developed from this first speck of living material, beings with intelligent self-consciousness eventually emerged through the process of biological evolution.

The most successful of these creatures—members of the species *homo sapiens*—were intelligent enough, and survived as a species for long enough, to allow a complex culture to develop, in which the whole of this development from the Big Bang onwards came to be understood with remarkable scope and precision. For the physical scientists among these humans, the character of the

recognized—as scientists do now—that time could not exist "prior to" the existence of the cosmos, since time is a part of the cosmos and not something separate from it.

inanimate universe came to be seen as the straightforward result of the laws of physics acting on the initial conditions that existed after the Big Bang. For the biologists among them, the species of their planet, including the one to which they themselves belonged, came to be seen as the result of processes just as naturalistic as those described by the physical scientists. What Newton had begun in the seventeenth century had, by our own time, become an astonishingly robust and beautiful explanatory framework for the development of the entire non-living cosmos. What Darwin had begun in the nineteenth century had, similarly, become an astonishingly beautiful and robust framework for understanding the development of the entire living world.

We cannot, of course, regard the picture that the sciences currently present as a definitive one, for the intellectual adventure goes on. New observations will inevitably present new challenges,[3] and even without these there are still many "loose ends" to be tied up. These loose ends relate to what the philosopher of science, Imre Lakatos, has called called "auxiliary hypotheses."[4] These he sees as different to the "core theories" to which they relate, in that the latter usually remain unchallenged, while the former continue to evoke debate among scientists and give rise to competing research programs, which are often aimed at reinforcing one of these hypotheses at the expense of others.[5]

[3]At the time of writing, the astronomical observations associated with the hypotheses of "dark matter" and "dark energy" provide a good example of how this can happen, sometimes indicating (as we shall see presently) that a scientific revolution, of the kind analyzed by the philosopher of science, Thomas Kuhn, may become necessary; see Thomas Kuhn, *The Structure of Scientific Revolutions* (Chicago: University of Chicago Press, 1962).

[4]See, e.g., Imre Lakatos, "Falsification and the Methodology of Scientific Research Programmes," in I. Lakatos and A. Musgrave, eds., *Criticism and the Growth of Knowledge* (Cambridge: Cambridge University Press, 1970), 91ff.

[5]An important example of this lies in interpretations of evolutionary

In addition to this kind of insight, we need to acknowledge that we cannot entirely rule out a future scientific revolution in the sense in which another philosopher of science, Thomas Kuhn, has used that term.[6] The universe envisaged by Newton has already been incorporated, through such a revolution, into the wider vision of Albert Einstein, and the Neo-Darwinism of Darwin's successors may one day also be incorporated into a wider vision.[7]

Even when we take these philosophical insights into account, however, we need to recognize that we live in a world in which the majority of scientists and philosophers of science—Christian believers as well as others—are confident that future developments of scientific understanding will confirm, rather than overturn, the basis of our current understanding, at least to the extent that a fundamentally naturalistic picture will remain.

Where the Christian believers among these scientists and philosophers differ from their atheistic colleagues lies, not in their

theory. The core theory is unquestioned in biological circles but aspects of its associated auxiliary hypotheses have given rise to significant debates. But, as Stephen Jay Gould once said—in response to criticisms of the core theory based on the fact that he and Richard Dawkins disagreed on aspects of its interpretation—to see these disagreements as having implications for the validity of that core theory is inane. See Stephen Connor, "Eminent Biologist Hits Back at the Creationists Who 'Hijacked' His Theory for Their Own Ends," *The Independent* (London: 9 April 2002): 3.

[6]This will be discussed in Chapter 4.

[7]Indeed, epigenetic factors are already being recognized by biologists in a way that represents, at the very least, a significant revision of the Neo-Darwinism of only a generation ago. In very simplified terms, epigenetics is the study of mechanisms that will switch genetic influence on and off. Recognition of these mechanisms has altered the tendency in earlier generations of geneticists to see the effects of genes in a deterministic way. It is now recognized that there may be a complex interaction between genes and the wholes of which they are part, including environmental factors, with characteristics that are not gene-determined being transmissible from one generation to the next.

attitude towards the validity of this scientific picture, but in their evaluation of its ability to explain everything that can be explained. For atheists, there are simply no answers to questions such as "Why is there something rather than nothing?"[8] or "Why does the cosmos have the extraordinary potential to produce beings like us?" Because science cannot answer these questions, these atheists sometimes assume that these are not legitimate questions at all.

This belief that only a scientific methodology can provide legitimate understanding is, as we have noted, sometimes called *scientism*. This scientism is not, however, intrinsic to the pursuit of scientific understanding, and many non-believing scientists, as well as religiously-inclined ones, see it as deeply flawed. What distinguishes the believing scientists from those of their agnostic colleagues who share their criticism of scientism is that they believe that we can, at least in principle, legitimately offer a theological interpretation of scientific theories. This need not, they stress, involve denying those theories' validity as an account of the mechanisms through which the cosmos operates and has developed. Rather, they assume that it is possible to speak about the purpose of that development, and to see God as the one who lies behind that development and is at the heart of it.

Thus, for example, one of these believing scientists, a Western religious scholar with an academic background in biochemistry, has written what he calls a *Genesis for the Third Millennium*, which goes as follows:

[8]Some seem to believe that this question may be answered in terms of the scientific speculation that the physical world, as we can observe it, came into being through fluctuations in a quantum vacuum. But a quantum vacuum is not "nothing" in any but the trivial sense that it is not made up of material particles. Since it obeys laws of nature, it is already clearly "something."

There was God, and God was All-That Was. God's love over-
flowed and God said, "Let Other be. And Let there be Laws
for what it is and what it can be—and let it explore its possibilities and potentialities." And there was Other, a field of
energy, which exploded as the Universe . . . Five billion years
ago, one star in one galaxy—our Sun—attracted round it matter as planets. One of them was our Earth. There the assem-
bly of atoms and the temperature became just right to allow
some molecules to become large and complex enough to make
copies of themselves—the first specks of life. Life multiplied
and burst into many forms. Mammals appeared and began to
develop complex brains, which enabled them to learn. Among
these were creatures who lived in trees. From these our first
ancestors derived and then . . . the first men and women
appeared. They began to know about themselves and what
they were doing—they were not only conscious but also self-
conscious. The first word, the first laugh were heard. The first
paintings were made. The first sense of destiny beyond—with
the first signs of hope, for they buried their dead with ritual.
The first prayers were made to the One who made All-That-Is
and All-That-Is-Becoming. The first experiences of goodness,
beauty and truth—but also of their opposites—human beings
had free will.[9]

This account was not, we should note, written in an attempt
to replace the scriptural creation accounts. It was designed
simply to supplement them, providing a kind of exegesis that
accepts both our current scientific understanding and the religious truths that the scriptural accounts embody. It was presented, in fact, as part of a sermon, and it represents an attempt

[9]Arthur Peacocke, sermon given in the chapel of King's College, Cambridge, 2 March 1997, quoted with Peacocke's permission in Christopher C.
Knight, *Wrestling with the Divine*, 11f.

to do something that many see as highly important in our scientific age: to develop a theological interpretation of our current scientific understanding so as to incorporate all the resonances of the scriptural understanding of the dependence of the cosmos on its Creator.

The author of this sermon, Arthur Peacocke, was one of three scholars—the others being Ian Barbour and John Polkinghorne—who dominated Western Christian studies of the relationship between science and theology in the late twentieth century These three are sometimes described as the *scientist-theologians,* since they all began their adult lives, not as theological scholars, but as trained scientists, so that they were able bring to the theological task an informed knowledge of the sciences that was then rare among those involved in that task.

Some religious fundamentalists believe that there is a major problem associated with the work of these scientist-theologians and of the many scholars in this field who have followed them. The perceived problem is that these scholars read the Genesis accounts of God's action as Creator in a way that sets aside any literalist interpretation of those accounts. The world, these scholars insist, was not created in the way the fundamentalists insist it was: through a series of separate divine acts that occurred only a few thousand years ago.

The reason for seeing an insuperable problem with fundamentalist readings of this kind is that there is overwhelming scientific evidence for a continuous process that has occurred over a timescale of billions of years. This evidence makes quite untenable the fundamentalist view that the world was brought into being only a few thousand years ago and since then has remained fundamentally unchanged. The untenable nature of this "young earth creationism" view is evident, not only from the combination of the astronomical evidence that we have noted and the fossil evidence for life's having had a very long and complex evolutionary history; in addition, there is the geological evidence of the great age of the earth, which fits very well with the astronomical evidence.[10] (The early forms of this geological evidence in fact provided the first real challenge to young earth creationism, leading many early nineteenth-century Christians to understand the Genesis account of the "days" of creation as referring to æons of great length.)

Despite all this overwhelming scientific evidence, however, the belief that the earth is very much older than a few thousand years is still seen by some Protestant fundamentalists (and even by a few Orthodox) as theologically unacceptable. The Protestant fundamentalists who hold this view rely on their reading of the Bible. The Orthodox fundamentalists who hold the same view are slightly different because they tend to put less stress on the Bible than on the Fathers of the Church. Many of these Fathers, they argue, believed the earth to be only a few thousand years old, and therefore we Orthodox—with our stress on Tradition—should not depart from that view.

But this is to misread our Tradition, since the Fathers of the Church themselves had differing views on how the creation accounts should be read. They had no reason, it is true, to believe the earth to be very old, since the science of their time was rudimentary. Nevertheless, as we shall see, several of them did read the Genesis accounts in a non-fundamentalist way, seeing the creation, not as a series of acts, but as a single, instantaneous act. Indeed, a few of them, like St Augustine of Hippo and St Basil the Great, even hinted at a kind of evolutionary scenario, suggesting

[10]This astronomical evidence indicates that the cosmos is actually about three times older than the Earth itself, and this is understandable because, in its early stages, the universe contained no stars, and our own Sun is not one of the earliest generation of these stars. If it had been, it could not have had planets containing carbon, which was necessary for life to begin.

that some things that we now experience existed in the beginning only as potentialities—"seeds" that God had planted—which would only later come to fruition.

The Fathers were able to offer this kind of reading of the scriptural account because they recognized that the early Christian philosopher, Origen, was correct in arguing that certain passages of Scripture, "by means of seeming history, though the incidents never occurred, figuratively reveal certain mysteries." This saying of Origen was, in fact, quoted directly[11] in an anthology of his writings compiled by Saints Gregory of Nazianzus and Basil the Great, in order to emphasize the view that Orthodox Christians are not necessarily tied to the literal meaning of any scriptural text. If there is good reason to doubt the literal, historical truth of some particular passage, they believed, then it is permissible to set aside that passage's literal meaning and focus on its way of teaching moral or mystical truths.

Because the science of their time did not make it necessary, not all of the Church's Fathers applied this insight to the creation accounts, and some of them undoubtedly did read the Genesis accounts as simple history. Some of them, however, did apply Origen's insights to these texts.[12] St Gregory of Nyssa, for example, saw the days of creation, not in terms of the kind of temporal sequence that a literalist reading would indicate, but in terms of an instantaneous creation. He saw the "days" of creation as delineating a philosophical truth that is reinforced for us now by

[11]*The Philokalia of Origen: A Compilation of Selected Passages From Origen's Works Made by St Gregory of Nazianzus and St Basil of Caesarea*, tr. George Lewis (Edinburgh: T & T Clark, 1911), 18.

[12]For a good general study of the different readings of the Genesis creation accounts in the patristic period, see Peter C. Bouteneff, *Beginnings: Ancient Christian Readings of the Biblical Creation Narratives* (Grand Rapids: Baker Academic, 2008).

the sciences of our own time: that human life is rooted in animal life and animal life in inorganic processes.[13]

If patristic writers like Gregory could put aside the literal meaning of the Genesis accounts, then surely so can we. Yet, if we acknowledge this we must also remember that, as Orthodox Christians, we must ensure that the process of developing a non-literalist interpretation does not involve abandoning any of the theological insights that were central to the patristic witness. For this reason, we must be careful that we do not uncritically follow Western scholars in our exploration of how modern scientific insights may be seen as consonant with Christian faith. In particular, as we shall see, we must recognize that the approach of almost all Western Christian scholars who have participated in the science-theology dialogue manifest major blind-spots in relation to patristic understanding.

These blind-spots have given rise to a widespread failure to incorporate five important aspects of the Fathers' approach into their thinking. These are:

(i) their understanding of the use and limitations of theological and scientific languages;

(ii) their christological focus in understanding the concept of creation;

(iii) their understanding of the role of humanity in bringing God's purposes to fulfilment;

(iv) their sense that the empirical world can be understood theologically only when "the world to come" is taken fully into account;

---

[13]St Gregory of Nyssa, *On The Making of Man* 8.5.

(v) their sense that material entities should be understood less in materialist terms than in relation to the "mind of God."

We shall examine all of these facets of the patristic witness in what follows. At this stage, however, it may be useful to note that the last of these five is of particular importance. This is because it relates to the way in which, in the work of many Western theological scholars, there is a tendency to look simplistically at the scientific understanding of the world. They see it—in a way which is commonly assumed by scientists but which is not entailed by science—as pointing to the existence of an autonomous set of entities and of laws of nature that God must manipulate "from the outside" if his will is to be fulfilled. This sense of God's being on the outside of an essentially autonomous universe is something that is in stark contrast to our Orthodox approach. For, while maintaining the distinction between the creation and the Creator is central to our Orthodox understanding, we see God as being at the very heart of all created entities and of processes. (This is especially the case, as we shall see, in relation to what St Maximos the Confessor calls the *logoi* of created things and to what St Gregory Palamas calls the divine *energies*.) This means that we must look with a critical eye at the understanding of how God acts in the world that is still predominant in the Western science-theology dialogue. This issue is, as we shall see, one of many that make our Orthodox theology of creation distinctive in relation to assumptions that are dominant within that dialogue, and we need to have a proper understanding of this distinctiveness in order to avoid the distortions and blind spots that have arisen among some Western Christians in their response to science.

chapter two

ORTHODOX WRITERS AND THE SCIENCES

I n light of the historical and theological background outlined in Chapter 1, it is illuminating to explore how, over the centuries, Orthodox authors have responded to the sciences of their own time. The first thing that perhaps needs to be clarified here is that we need to move beyond the common and mistaken notion that science and theology have always been in conflict. In practice, there has often been a much more complex relationship, and while this is now widely appreciated in the Western context (at least among serious historians)[1] there is perhaps less appreciation among Orthodox that the same has been true of our own community. Here, therefore, we should be grateful to the Greek historian, Efthymios Nicolaidis, for his recent overview of this complexity in the Orthodox world.[2]

[1]Among the general population in the West there is still a widespread belief that science and religion have always been opposed to one another. For an attempt to dispel some of the myths surrounding this belief, see Ronald L. Numbers, ed., *Galileo Goes to Jail: And Other Myths About Science and Religion* (Harvard: Harvard University Press, 2009).

[2]Efthymios Nicolaidis, *Science and Eastern Orthodoxy: From the Greek Fathers to the Age of Globalization* (Baltimore: Johns Hopkins University Press, 2011), explores much that is outlined in this chapter (at least up to modern times). As the author rightly observes, his book constitutes the first general account of the interrelationships between science and Orthodox

One of the things that Nicolaidis highlights is the way in which the Orthodox approach and experience have not been the same as those of Western Christianity. In particular, he stresses that, in medieval times, the scientific tradition of the classical world was never forgotten in the Hellenic world in the way that it was in Western Christendom, where it needed to be rediscovered in the later Middle Ages through transmission of texts and interpretation from the Muslim world. The Christians of the Hellenic world—up to and even beyond the rise of modern science—encountered the sciences primarily through "the perpetuation of a tradition of teaching ancient Greek science in the Greek language, sometimes as reviewed and modified by the Greek fathers of the school of Alexandria."[3] This Alexandrian patristic legacy meant that, in the Greek-speaking world, science could be—and often was—seen as part of the Christian heritage, and pride could be taken in its Hellenic roots.

Another difference between Eastern and Western Christian communities was that in the East arguments about the use of science in articulating theology tended to be between different groups of Christians, and were less complicated by arguments between

Christianity over the centuries, and as such it is, as he notes, "necessarily summary and partial" (xi). In particular, although he does indicate something of the way in which the Russian church has often opposed "scientific culture, whether Byzantine or otherwise" (140), he frankly recognizes that his book "largely neglects the Slavic Orthodox Church, which followed its own course and deserves its own history" (xii). The book in fact focuses very largely on the experience of the Christians of the Hellenic world, and does not describe some of the more positive developments of recent decades, which have witnessed the beginnings of a very constructive dialogue between science and Orthodox Christianity. Nevertheless, the book provides an excellent account of those regions and periods that it does cover, and it is essential reading for those who wish to look in more detail at the historical developments outlined in this chapter.

[3]Nicolaidis, *Science and Eastern Orthodoxy*, x.

Christianity and its challengers. Conflicts—when they existed— "were not 'science versus Christianity' but rather ecclesiastical conflicts that traversed the whole society and consequently also implicated the sciences by always coming back to the importance of secular knowledge and the possibility for humankind to conceive the Creation through science."[4]

This recognition of differences between groups of Eastern Christians is important to us because it emphasizes that any attitude towards science that we find in a particular Orthodox author does not necessarily form part of the consensus that we Orthodox see as the basis of our Tradition. Whenever we encounter any comment about a matter related to science in the work of an Orthodox author, we need to put that comment into its historical context. Occasionally such a comment may turn out to represent the Orthodox consensus of the period in which that writer lived. In other cases, however, we will find that it represents no more than *a* standpoint, with which other Orthodox Christians of that period disagreed.

Indeed, we must be careful, not only in our reading of authors of medieval and modern times, but even in claiming a patristic consensus on these matters. The Fathers themselves exhibited differences of emphasis despite all that they had in common. Differences in the works of Saints Basil the Great and Gregory of Nyssa, for example, indicate how questions about the limits of reason and the sources of valid knowledge were already at least implicitly part of Christian debate in the fourth century.[5] More generally, the differences between the schools of Antioch and Alexandria in this early period were considerable, with the former tending much more towards a literalist reading of Scripture than the latter.[6]

[4]Nicolaidis, *Science and Eastern Orthodoxy*, x.

[5]Nicolaidis, *Science and Eastern Orthodoxy*, 1–23.

[6]It should perhaps be said that in the first two chapters of his book, Nicolaidis—whose historical expertise relates primarily to a much later

The scientific understanding of some later Byzantine philosopher-theologians, such as John Philoponus,[7] was clearly rooted in the Alexandrian tradition. The controversy between him and the Antiochian-influenced Cosmas Indicopleustes illustrates the way in which, in this period, the Alexandrian party could accept the Hellenic science of their time with only minor modifications, while the Antiochians tended to be wary of it. Although both of these men were later (and for other reasons)[8] regarded as heretics, this did not prevent their cosmological views from being spread into the Byzantine Middle Ages. The Alexandrian view—that the phenomena of nature are due to the principles of physics that God has installed in his creation—were often, throughout this period, challenged by the successors of the Antiochians. Especially among monks and the lower clergy, there was a tendency for the natural philosophy of the ancients to be replaced by a view in which angels were seen as responsible for all the phenomena of nature.[9]

period—does not give as nuanced an account of either the Cappadocians or of the influences of Alexandrian and Antiochian thought as one immersed in the literature of this early period might have done. (In particular, he does not sufficiently stress that the best Antiochian thought was not as simplistic as the interpretation of it that characterized the work of some who manifested its tendency to read the Scriptures in a literalist manner). Nevertheless, his main point—that significant differences of emphasis on the question of legitimate sources of theological knowledge existed from an early period—is clearly a valid one. As the rest of his book indicates in a persuasive way, Hellenic Christians of the Middle Ages and of the modern period continued to struggle with the kinds of issues that this early period witnessed. Despite the existence of a vibrant scientific tradition during much of this period—often fostered by the higher clergy—this tradition usually had its opponents, who in some periods became the dominant force within the church.

[7]Nicolaidis, *Science and Eastern Orthodoxy*, 24–39.

[8]Philoponus was condemned for his belief that the Trinity is not of one essence; Cosmas because of his association with the theological teachings of Theodore of Mopsuestia.

[9]Nicolaidis, *Science and Eastern Orthodoxy*, 39.

Perhaps the first period in which the old Hellenic scientific tradition was almost eclipsed was that which coincided with the iconoclast controversies of the seventh and eighth centuries. In this period, scholarly scientific literature fell into decline and—partly through the popularity of unsophisticated hagiographic or miraculous texts—a kind of simplistic popular science tended to take its place.[10] Nevertheless, it was not long after the iconodule victory in the seventh ecumenical council of AD 787 that a new and more positive phase of the relationship between science and theology began, with a revival of science characterized by the work of people like John the Grammarian and Leo the Mathematician. This led to new emphases, and—as the approaches of Michael Psellos and John Italos indicate—there was a transition from an older Byzantine humanism to something more distinctly medieval.[11]

The subjugation of much of the Hellenic world to Frankish rule after the fourth crusade of 1204 might have been expected to extinguish this new flame, but in fact this did not happen everywhere. In the Empire of Nicaea, in particular, the flame was kept alight by Nicephorus Blemmydes.[12] Later, when reunion with Rome was regarded by some as essential to hold at bay the military threat from the Ottomans, it was seen as necessary for senior ecclesiastics—who would have to negotiate in a erudite way with delegates from Rome—to be familiar with secular as well as spiritual disciplines. As a result, the Patriarchal School in Constantinople felt the need to employ sophisticated scholars like George Pachymeres, whose *Quadrivium* constituted an advanced manual of the science of his day.[13]

[10]Nicolaidis, *Science and Eastern Orthodoxy*, 40–54.
[11]Nicolaidis, *Science and Eastern Orthodoxy*, 55–68.
[12]Nicolaidis, *Science and Eastern Orthodoxy*, 69–80.
[13]Nicolaidis, *Science and Eastern Orthodoxy*, 81–92.

In certain ways, the fourteenth century witnessed new versions of the old debates between those who saw secular knowledge as an important component of the theological scholar's task and those who saw it as irrelevant or even as a hindrance. While in much of the earlier debate this latter group had focused on the knowledge that they believed to have been revealed through Scripture, there now came to the fore a *hesychast* focus on "direct" spiritual knowledge, with the pro-hesychast views of St Gregory Palamas eventually prevailing.[14]

It is arguable, however, that this hesychast victory had different effects in different parts of the Orthodox world. Palamas' views were not, in fact, dismissive of secular learning, and the kind of dismissal that became characteristic of some in the hesychast party seems to have had more influence in the Slav world than in the Hellenic one. (Indeed, as Nicolaidis notes, the success of the hesychast party may be seen as "the spiritual origin of the complicated relations between science and Russian society and also constituted the ideological basis of Slavic mysticism."[15]) In the Hellenic world, science continued to flourish, with astronomy in particular being encouraged by church leaders.

After the fall of Constantinople to the Ottomans in 1453, not only did the old Byzantine educational system effectively cease to exist, but in addition the church hierarchy rather abruptly distanced itself from secular learning.[16] For some considerable time it was mainly to Italy that Greeks had to look if they were to receive the kind of secular education that had been previously available to them nearer home. In the sixteenth century, however, when a community of Orthodox scholars tried to formulate a new discourse on the sciences, it was torn between "its

---

[14]Nicolaidis, *Science and Eastern Orthodoxy*, 93–105.
[15]Nicolaidis, *Science and Eastern Orthodoxy*, 104.
[16]Nicolaidis, *Science and Eastern Orthodoxy*, 119–29.

privileged links with Italian science"[17] and the militant anti-Roman Catholic sentiment of the great majority of their fellow Greeks.

In Russia, an earlier, hesychast-inspired suspicion of science was modified in the seventeenth century, partly because of the need to counter Jesuit influence in Russian-controlled territories and partly because of Hellenic interest in the political possibilities of Russian political power. Here, the activities in Russia of Chrysanthos Notaras, later Patriarch of Jerusalem, were of considerable significance.[18] Chrysanthos in practice departed from the older scientific tradition of Orthodox humanism, which had tended to see only Hellenic science as valid. Now, the "new sciences" of Western Europe were presented (rather cautiously) to the Orthodox world by a man of impeccable ecclesiastic credentials. Together with educational developments, this led to increasing acceptance of these new sciences.

After 1789, however, the effects of the French revolution led to an increasingly reactionary stance among influential church people, not only in relation to political and social ideas associated with the Enlightenment, but also to what was seen as their scientific underpinning.[19] This led to a situation in the Greek world that still exists to some extent today, with philosophical and theological issues sometimes being associated with—and at least partially obscured by—political and social ones.[20]

This historical insight—about the recent intertwining of theological, social, and political issues in the responses of different

[17]Nicolaidis, *Science and Eastern Orthodoxy*, 127.

[18]Nicolaidis, *Science and Eastern Orthodoxy*, 140–50.

[19]Nicolaidis, *Science and Eastern Orthodoxy*, 151–168. Even important figures like Eugenios Voulgaris, Nicolaidis notes, were shaken in their adherence to the new sciences and to the associated philosophical and political ideas of the Enlightenment.

[20]Nicolaidis, *Science and Eastern Orthodoxy*, 169–192.

groups of Greek believers to science[21]—is important for our understanding. Especially when the evident parallels in other parts of the Orthodox world are taken into account, it underlines the fact that at least some of the criticism of scientific understanding that exists today among Orthodox Christians is based less on careful theological analysis of the issues than on an essentially reactionary agenda. Side by side with this reactionary agenda, however, there has emerged a rather different agenda, influenced by respected theologians such as Fr Dumitru Staniloae.[22] In this agenda, there is strong encouragement to express the rich Orthodox understanding of the relationship between the cosmos and its Creator in terms of the insights of modern science.

Orthodox responses to this encouragement are, however, still at an embryonic stage of development. In the Western theological community, a rich "science-theology dialogue" has existed for over half a century, and we must ask why it is that a comparable dialogue has only begun more recently in the Orthodox world, especially when we remember that the use of scientific insights was such a significant part of the patristic thinking that we see as the foundation for our theology. Is it explicable, perhaps, in terms of the influence of an unbalanced hesychastic stress on knowing

[21]Well within living memory, for example, as Nicolaidis recounts, "Kallinikos Karoussos (born Konstantinos, 1926–2008), later elected metropolitan of Piraeus, had collaborated with Christos Paraskevaidis (1939–2008), the future archbishop of Greece known as Christodoulos, in founding the Christian fraternity *Chrysopigi*. This aggressively fundamentalist fraternity fought against the teaching of evolution, while confusing evolution with Marxism . . . Kallinikos went on to found the Piraeus association of scientists in 1993, dedicated to fostering nationalist and anti-evolutionary ideas" (Nicolaidis, *Science and Eastern Orthodoxy*, 191).

[22]A useful survey of Staniloae's attitude is given in Doru Costache, "At the Crossroads of Contemporary Cosmology and the Patristic Worldview: Movement, Rationality and Purpose in Father Dumitru Staniloae," *Studii Teologice* (third series) 9.2 (2013): 141–64.

the creation through direct contemplative experience rather than on knowing about it through human reason? Or in terms, perhaps, of a tendency among some to stress the Orthodox orientation towards "Tradition" in such a way that current theology is seen as little more than a process of writing footnotes to patristic works?

However we judge these questions, we also perhaps need to take into account sociological factors comparable to those we have noted as characteristic of the Greek situation. Many Orthodox Christians outside the Greek world lived, until very recently, in situations in which they were inevitably influenced by the need to react against their governments' promulgation of the Marxist-Leninist version of atheism, with its supposed support from the sciences. This has meant that, even after the downfall of that ideology in their countries, many of them have tended, almost instinctively, to see science and atheism as having an intrinsic connection. In addition, at least some influential Orthodox in the West have developed a similar attitude for reasons that are susceptible to comparable sociological analysis. Especially if reacting against the recent "liberalization" of many of the mainstream Western forms of Christianity, they too may tend to associate science with the ideologies of those they perceive to be the enemies or diluters of faith.

If suspicion of science does exist among some Orthodox Christians, however, it should not be equated in its origins or effects with the superficially similar attitude of some of the fundamentalist Christians of the West. While the two groups may sometimes be comparable in sociological terms, their theological views are usually very different.

For example, scriptural interpretation is, as we have noted, strongly influenced in Orthodox circles by the way in which theologians of the patristic period—especially those in the Alexandrian tradition—often read the Old Testament Scriptures using an allegorical rather than a literal mode of interpretation. This means, for example, that the creation accounts in Genesis are not usually seen by Orthodox Christians as they are by those Protestant fundamentalists who insist that, because they are to be found in the Bible, they provide literal, "scientific" truths about the way in which the cosmos came into being.[23]

The reason for this is, as we have noted, that Orthodox Christians see the mystical truths conveyed by Scripture as central to its purpose, and are therefore not necessarily tied to the literal meaning of any scriptural text. If there is good reason to doubt the literal, historical truth of some particular passage, it is permissible to set aside that passage's literal meaning and focus on its way of teaching other, more profound truths. It is important to recognize this because there are still a few, within the Orthodox Church, who insist that a literalist interpretation that the creation accounts represents the patristic consensus and therefore must be seen as part of the Orthodox Tradition. As we have noted, however, to say this is simply to misrepresent (or possibly be ignorant of) the facts.

Another misrepresentation is the not-uncommon assertion that any kind of evolutionary theory is completely alien to the patristic understanding. An evolutionary scenario was, admittedly, unavailable to the Fathers on scientific grounds, which is perhaps why few of them suggested it. We should not forget, however, that some of them did hint at the possibility of a gradual unfolding of the potential of what God had created "in the beginning."

St Augustine of Hippo, for example, quite explicitly suggested a scenario that is distinctly reminiscent of evolutionary theory.

---

[23]An exception to this statement is to be found among a small number of Orthodox influenced by Protestant fundamentalism, a significant factor mainly in America.

46

God, he said, may have created potentialities in the creation which—like dormant "seeds"—only gradually came to fruition.[24] In a similar way, the understanding of St Basil the Great was that "God did not command the earth immediately to give forth seed and fruit, but to produce germs, to grow green, and to arrive at maturity in the seed; so that this first command teaches nature what she has to do in the course of the ages."[25]

For example, Basil explicitly sees the biblical phrase "Let the earth bring forth living creatures," not as something true only of the initial emergence of life, but as a present and constant reality. Using the mistaken science of his time—in which it was believed that not all animals are produced by parents—he cites grasshoppers, small insects, mice, frogs and eels as creatures that continue to come into existence spontaneously from the earth.[26] He seems, in fact, to see the earth as having been endowed from the beginning with all the powers necessary to realize the whole array of lifeforms intended by God to come into being in due course. Examining this and other aspects of the *Hexameron*, Howard van Till has concluded that "Basil expresses his conviction that although the Creator's word is spoken in an instant, the Creation's obedient response is extended in time." Indeed, Van Till goes on, at times Basil speaks "in language that seems almost to anticipate modern scientific concepts." [27]

[24]St Augustine, *The Literal Interpretation of Genesis.*

[25]St Basil the Great, *Hexameron* 5.5

[26]St Basil, *Hexameron* 9.2

[27]Howard van Till, "Basil, Augustine, and the Doctrine of Creation's Functional Integrity," *Science and Christian Belief* 8 (1996): 21–38. Van Till quotes here the important comment of Thomas F. Torrance (in his book *The Christian Frame of Mind*, [Colorado Springs: Helmers and Howard, 1989], 4) that while "commenting upon the Genesis account of creation through the majestic fiat of God: 'Let there be,' Basil pointed out that though acts of divine creation took place timelessly, the creative commands of God gave rise to orderly sequences and enduring structures in the world of time and

These patristic writers did not, of course, have in mind any-thing quite like modern evolutionary theory. Nevertheless, given the way in which they anticipated at least some aspects of that theory, it is unsurprising that advocates of that theory seem to be becoming more numerous in the Orthodox community. This trend has, moreover, been encouraged by the observations of some Orthodox patristic scholars that our Tradition does not preclude evolutionary insights.

Father Andrew Louth, for example, has commented that the writings of St Maximos the Confessor manifest the assump-tion that natures are fixed, just as did the all writings of his seventh century contemporaries. Nevertheless, Louth observes, Maximos' thought is still dynamic enough to be implicitly open "to the idea of evolution . . . as a way of expressing God's provi-dence" so that that his cosmic vision can "be re-thought in terms of modern science."[28] In a similarly helpful way, Panayiotis Nellas has commented—on grounds that we shall explore presently—that "the essence of man is not found in the matter from which he was created but in the archetype [the incarnate *Logos*] on the basis of which he was formed and towards which he tends." It is precisely for this reason, he goes on, that for the Ortho-dox understanding, "the theory of evolution does not create a problem . . . because the archetype is that which organizes, seals and gives shape to matter, and which simultaneously attracts it towards itself."[29]

Despite such assurances, however, there is as yet no consensus about how to formulate a contemporary Orthodox response to

space. It was thus that the voice of God in creation gave rise to laws of nature. Expressed the other way round, this means that all the laws of nature, all its intelligible order, are to be regarded as dependent on the word of God as their source and ground."

[28]Louth "The Cosmic Vision of Saint Maximos the Confessor," 189.
[29]Nellas, *Deification in Christ*, 33.

the sciences in general and to evolutionary theory in particular. Intellectual ferment in this area—characteristic of Western Christianity for several generations—has been rare in Orthodox circles until relatively recently. This rarity, coupled with the sociological factors already mentioned, means that a wide spectrum of views still exists.

At one end of the spectrum is the essentially anti-scientific attitude expressed by writers like Philip Sherrard and Father Seraphim Rose. Sherrard—a very perceptive writer in relation to many aspects of Orthodox theology—seems to have an extraordinary blind spot when it comes to understanding the nature of science. He fails to perceive any validity in the distinctions commonly made between technology and pure science and between science and scientism.[30] Rose effectively defends a kind of fundamentalism in relation to selected strands of the patristic literature.[31] This fundamentalism has been intelligently questioned, from within the Orthodox community, by George and Elizabeth Theokritoff, who rightly observe that Rose is "firmly convinced that 'the doctrine of evolution was invented . . . to account for the universe on the assumption that God either does not exist or is incapable of creating in six days or bringing the world into existence by his mere word' . . . and that Christians accept it only because they have fallen into the latter two of those assumptions." This quite fails to recognize, they go on, "that many Christians accept evolution for a reason of quite a different order: that while God is

---

[30]See, e.g., Philip Sherrard, *Human Image: World Image—The Death and Resurrection of Sacred Cosmology* (Ipswich: Golgonooza, 1992). It may be that Sherrard's blind spot in relation to science is related to the clear influence on his thinking of the "Traditionalist school" associated with the Islamic scholar, René Guénon, which has a similar blind spot.

[31]Seraphim Rose, *Genesis, Creation, and Early Man*, 2nd rev. ed. (Platina: St Herman of Alaska Brotherhood, 2011).

---

perfectly capable of creating everything in six days, the weight of evidence suggests that in point of fact he did not."[32]

Among Orthodox commentators, a more common view than the "conflict" one of Sherrard or Rose is that of those who—while not rejecting science—see science and theology as essentially independent of each other, so that they neither conflict nor interact. This view is sometimes the outcome of the kind of postmodernist perspective that we shall examine presently. Of the Orthodox exponents of this kind of postmodernist perspective, Christos Yannaras perhaps represents the most sophisticated philosophical position.

It is, however, Alexei Nesteruk who presents the most interesting "independence" argument from the perspective of one who (as a cosmologist) knows the sciences from the inside. While affirming science as a legitimate expression of the human spirit, Nesteruk tends to bypass questions about truth in science and theology, and about the consonance or dissonance between them, by interpreting both in terms of the philosophical approach known as phenomenology. Major themes in Orthodox theological thought can, he claims, be incorporated in this approach.[33]

One aspect of Nesteruk's understanding—which can be appreciated even by those who are not sympathetic towards his philosophical framework—is his insistence that science and theology both have roots in the human spirit. This means, he argues, that there cannot be a "dialogue" between them in some abstract sense. This is an interesting argument because the history of theological

[32]George Theokritoff and Elizabeth Theokritoff, "Genesis and Creation: Towards a Debate," *St Vladimir's Theological Quarterly* 26 (2002): 371.

[33]Alexei Nesteruk, *The Universe as Communion: Towards a Neo-Patristic Synthesis of Theology and Science* (London: T & T Clark, 2008). This work is full of important insights but suffers, in my judgment, from a rather selective approach to phenomenology and by a failure to appreciate fully the radical nature of Orthodoxy's apophatic understanding of language usage.

responses to the sciences indicates that it is only among those individuals for whom both science and theology are existentially important that anything fruitful emerges. Nesteruk's general approach is valuable, in my judgment, because it gives a sense of why this might be so.

Nevertheless, I believe that we need to move beyond this position to provide an assessment of the possibility of interaction between science and Orthodox theology that goes beyond the "independence" position. Assessments of this kind are to be found not only in my own thinking, but in that of people like Basarab Nicolescu and Gayle Woloschak, who do not reject the notion that science can help to provide a deeper understanding of theological themes.

Nicolescu—in his Romanian homeland in the 1990s—led the first major effort to develop a structured and widespread science-theology dialogue in a traditionally Orthodox country. His intellectual contribution has been based on essentially philosophical issues, in that he has taken bold and controversial strides to formulate a "transdisciplinary" approach that affects not only the science-theology dialogue but every area of human thought.[34] Woloschak—a professor of radiation oncology who also engages in theological teaching on the topic of science and theology—has both defended evolution in a theological context and done much to try to ensure that Orthodox ethical teaching is properly informed by scientific insights.[35]

My own contribution here has been to focus on theological issues (of the kind that the rest of this study will outline), arguing that the legitimate questions enunciated by participants in the

[34]Basarab Nicolescu, *Manifesto of Transdisciplinarity* (New York: State University of New York Press, 1992)

[35]See, e.g., Gayle E. Woloschak, *Faith, Science, Mystery* (Alhambra CA, St Sebastian Orthodox Press, 2018).

Western science-theology dialogue can be answered more satis-factorily when explored in terms of the Orthodox Tradition than they have been when examined in a Western Christian context.[36] In a tradition with such a rich and nuanced theology of creation, I have argued, it now seems likely—especially in view of the recent upsurge in interest—that a new and authentic unfolding of the Orthodox heritage will arise, and that this will be able to speak directly to the questions and concerns that are characteristic of our scientific age.

[36]See especially Christopher C. Knight, *The God of Nature: Incarnation and Contemporary Science* (Minneapolis: Fortress, 2007).

chapter three

NATURAL THEOLOGY
AND THE MIND OF
THE FATHERS

When faced with a theological question, we Orthodox Christians—with our focus on the Tradition of our Church—will inevitably ask how the biblical writers and those whom we revere as Fathers of the Church treated that question. But a question we are now faced with may not be one that presented itself in the biblical and patristic eras in the way that it does now. This means that we cannot always answer the questions we are faced with in terms of a simple statement that "the biblical perspective and the patristic consensus are such and such." Rather, we are forced to look at these ancient writings more carefully, asking how—if the Fathers had been in the position we are now in—they would have treated the issues that now arise.

This need to ask questions about methodology is particularly the case when we come to questions arising from the sciences, since the Fathers' scientific understanding—often quoted in their writings—was very much of their own era. Their scientific beliefs were, by and large, the common beliefs of the educated people of their time and these were, quite simply, often wrong.[1] (St Basil,

[1]Several of the Fathers, for example, either believed in a flat earth or—if they accepted what was then known scientifically about the spherical shape

for example, bases a theological argument—about the divine command that the earth should bring forth living creatures—at least partly on the belief that "We see mud alone produce eels; they do not proceed from an egg, nor in any other manner, it is the earth alone which gives them birth."[2])

Recognizing these limitations to the Fathers' scientific beliefs, we Orthodox cannot simply study those beliefs with the assumption that we are bound to believe the same as they did. Rather, we must ask more general questions about the the Fathers' use of science, and then try to apply what we have learned to our own situation.

This approach is consonant with the Orthodox understanding of Tradition since this understanding is not—as some seem to believe—simply about conserving the past. As Metropolitan Kallistos of Diokleia has put it, Tradition "is not static but dynamic, not a dead acceptance of the past but a living discovery of the Holy Spirit in the present. Tradition, while inwardly changeless (for God does not change) is constantly assuming new forms, which supplement the old without superseding them."[3] In working out the implications of this kind of understanding, it is important to remember that something that has been said by one (or even several) of the Fathers is not necessarily part of the Orthodox Tradition. As we have already noted, Metropolitan Kallistos has wisely pointed out the need to "separate Patristic wheat from Patristic chaff."[4]

Here, it is important to acknowledge that when the Fathers cited the scientific opinions of their time, they were focusing on

of our planet—were happy to repeat the common belief of their time that human life is necessarily limited to the earth's northern hemisphere.

[2]St Basil the Great, *Hexameron* 9.2.

[3]Timothy Ware, *The Orthodox Church*, rev. ed. (Harmondsworth: Penguin, 1993), 198.

[4]Ware, *The Orthodox Church*, 212.

theology and not directly on science. Their theology—even when it was illustrated by, or expressed in terms of, their scientific beliefs—never relied on those beliefs. Rather—as we have seen in the case of St Basil—they used the science of their time, together with the philosophical vocabulary that was available to them, to analyze and to speak about the *religious* truths of the Christian revelation in a way that could speak directly to the people of their age. It is—as we shall see in more detail presently—the body of these *religious* truths that constitutes the Orthodox Tradition.

To understand precisely what these religious truths are requires a recognition that the scientific and philosophical frameworks that the Fathers used did sometimes have an effect on the way they expressed their beliefs, and thus on the doctrinal inheritance that we have received from them. While the acts of God in history, as recounted in the Scriptures, were central to their thinking and provided the prime basis for their reflection on God's revelation of himself, the Fathers implicitly recognized that the scriptural accounts are not self-interpreting. (If they had been self-interpreting, then heresies could not have arisen.) In developing a mode of interpretation adequate to understand God's revelation of himself in history, they made use of the philosophy and science of their time, doing so in part by expanding the kind of *natural theology* that already existed in a rudimentary form in the classical philosophical tradition. Serious study of the Fathers, with the aim of appropriating the religious truths that they expounded, needs therefore to look carefully at the natural theology that they developed.

The term *natural theology* is used to describe what may be known about God, not through reflection on divine revelation in historical acts, but through intrinsic human capacities such as the ability to reflect philosophically and to infer conclusions from the way the world seems to be. It is a term that is sometimes avoided among Orthodox scholars, partly because it has often been understood in terms of Western developments in the period after the split between Orthodoxy and the Christianity of the West. In speaking of a properly Orthodox natural theology, therefore, we must explicitly exclude these post-schism Western developments, which included an increasing focus on attempts at logical "proofs" of God's existence[5] and a growing sense that a firm separation should be made between natural and supernatural revelation.[6] Nevertheless, the term *natural theology* may still—if it is understood more broadly[7]—legitimately be applied to aspects of the Orthodox Tradition, provided that the different trajectories taken by Christianity in its Eastern and Western forms are properly understood.

Crucial to understanding these different trajectories is recognizing the way in which the Orthodox notion of original sin is not the Augustinian one that has so strongly influenced much of Western theology. Orthodoxy does not see the image of God in humanity as having been completely destroyed through human rebellion against God, but simply as having been distorted. This means that

[5]In the medieval period these supposed proofs were essentially rooted in the Western scholastic approach and were philosophical in character. In the early modern period, as we shall note presently, they tended to focus on the character of the world as perceived by the sciences, arguing that the world was evidently the product of an intelligent designer.

[6]Such a separation is, as Fr Dumitru Staniloae has stressed, quite alien to the Orthodox Tradition, which never makes such a separation, and often—as in the work of St Maximos the Confessor—seems to see the latter simply as "the historical embodiment of the former." See Dumitru Staniloae, *The Experience of God: Orthodox Dogmatic Theology*, vol. 1: *Revelation and Knowledge of the Triune God* (Brookline: Holy Cross Orthodox Press, 1994), 1.

[7]This broad approach has been characteristic of most recent discussion, though up to the end of the twentieth century this was often not the case. For an example of the broader approach, see the essays in Russell Re Manning, ed., *The Oxford Handbook of Natural Theology* (Oxford: Oxford University Press, 2013).

for the Orthodox understanding, the created, "natural" capacity to know God at an intuitive level—though partially eclipsed in "fallen"[8] human nature—has not been effectively obliterated.[9]

Some Western traditions—especially those influenced by late-medieval scholasticism—have tended to see the fallenness of human nature as diminishing our discursive reasoning capacity less than it has diminished other human capacities. This led, in the late medieval and early modern periods, to a kind of Western natural theology that stressed supposedly "logical" arguments for the existence of God. Such attempts at logical arguments are, admittedly, sometimes to be found in Orthodox authors. (There are elements of them in the patristic writings and they have, as we shall note, reappeared in our own era.) Nevertheless, Orthodoxy's notion of the fallen nature of humanity has usually meant that its natural theology has tended to move in the opposite direction to

[8]As we shall see presently, although Orthodox theology puts much emphasis on our "fallen" nature, it does not necessarily see the origin of this nature in a "historical" fall, but at least sometimes interprets the biblical account of this fall in the Book of Genesis as in some sense indicating a meta-historical reality.

[9]This difference between East and West is particularly marked when we examine Calvinism. Calvin did, admittedly, have a sense of what he called the *sensus divinitatis* (which has become well known among philosophers in recent years because of its importance for Alvin Plantinga's development of "reformed epistemology"). This intrinsic human capacity for knowing God is, however, viewed by Calvin through the filter of something that represents an expansion of the Augustinian notion of original sin that is central to his thinking: his notion of *utter depravity*. This depravity means, for Calvin, that although the *sensus divinitatis* exists as an aspect of our created being, there is no one in whom it "ripens" (*Institutes of the Christian Religion* 1.4.1) so that "by itself it produces only the worst fruits" (1.4.4). This attitude contrasts markedly with the strand of Orthodox thinking that has its roots in St Justin Martyr's argument that even those who lived before the historical incarnation of the divine *Logos* could, through the love of wisdom, be sufficiently connected to that *Logos* to be, in a sense, already Christian (Justin Martyr, *First Apology* 46).

this scholastic approach. It has stressed that the unaided human reason—necessarily working with unprovable premises which may be mistaken—is potentially misleading unless underpinned by spiritual discernment that can provide an authentic foundation on which to build. As a result, it has tended to focus, in its natural theology, on other, more intuitive human capacities related to this discernment.[10]

One of the reasons for Orthodoxy's stress on something in human nature deeper than discursive reasoning is that our theology is characteristically an experiential one. Its approach is *mystical*—not in the sense of being anti-rational, but in a more complex sense. As Vladimir Lossky has put it, Christian dogma—often appearing at first as "an unfathomable mystery"—is something that should be approached by Orthodox "in such a fashion that instead of assimilating the mystery to our mode of understanding, we should, on the contrary, look for a profound change, an inner transformation of the spirit, enabling us to experience it mystically."[11]

Behind this approach lies the way in which Orthodoxy sees knowledge of God as being based, first and foremost, on contemplation (*theōria* in Greek): the perception or vision of the highest human faculty, the "intellect" (*nous*). This intellect is not the same as the discursive reasoning faculty (*dianoia)*, which latter is understood as functioning properly in theological analysis only if based on the spiritual knowledge (*gnōsis*) obtainable through

[10]Thus, for example, following the example of St John Chrysostom, Orthodox thinkers have sometimes invoked the concept of *natural law* in their thinking about ethics. But while some have explored parallels between natural and scriptural law in a way that may be compared to aspects of the scholastic development of the Western natural law tradition, the Orthodox approach to natural law has tended, in general, to stress the divinely-given nature of conscience rather than the sort of logical reasoning from observations of the world that was characteristic of the scholastic tradition.

[11]Vladimir Lossky, *The Mystical Theology of the Eastern Church* (Cambridge: James Clarke, 1957), 8.

the intellect. When this spiritual knowledge is present, there arises an understanding of the importance of *apophaticism*: the awareness that words can never circumscribe the realities to which they point. As part of this awareness, there is an acceptance of a degree of apparent logical inconsistency that secular philosophy would usually reject. (This apparent inconsistency is sometimes referred to as *antinomy*.)

As Vladimir Lossky has put it, "theology will never be abstract, working through concepts, but contemplative: raising the mind to those realities which pass all understanding. This is why the dogmas of the Church often present themselves as antinomies . . . It is not a question of suppressing the antinomy by adapting dogma to our understanding, but of change of heart and mind enabling us to attain to the contemplation of the reality which reveals itself to us as it raises us to God, and unites us, according to our several capacities, to Him."[12]

In relation to the cosmos, this is held to mean that the intellect—when purified by divine grace—provides not knowledge *about* the creation, expressed in verbal or mathematical terms. Rather, it provides a *direct* apprehension or spiritual perception of the inner essences or principles (*logoi*) of all the components of the cosmos. It is only when the functioning of the reasoning faculty is in accord with this immediate and intuitive experience that it can, according to Orthodox teaching, function adequately in theological analysis. (It is not for nothing that a theologian is, in the Orthodox understanding, not simply a believer who is a clear thinker, but is also—and mainly—"one who prays."[13])

---

[12]Lossky, *Mystical Theology*, 43 . He sees the doctrine of the Trinity as a prime example of antinomy in Orthodox thinking, since it embraces an understanding in which God is both one and three—something which secular philosophy would usually see as incoherent.

[13]This widespread saying seems to be based primarily on a passage by Evagrius Ponticus (*On Prayer* 60).

It is for this reason, I believe, that we need to be wary of the kind of argument now being advocated by Richard Swinburne—a convert to Orthodoxy—which is based on the kind of natural theology that arises from the application of analytical philosophy to religious concepts.[14] My reservations about his work are not based on a denial that his arguments have an important apologetic function, nor are they based on a belief those arguments are in any sense illogical. Rather, they are based on the fact that they arise from an essentially Western understanding of how philosophy functions in religious thinking. Any sense that the functioning of the discursive, rational faculty must be based on the functioning of the enlightened *nous* is absent. Moreover, even at a purely philosophical level, it is arguable that Swinburne's approach cannot be "purely" logical because in practice he gives different "weights" to his own arguments and to his opponents' counterarguments, and this involves a process that is ultimately intuitive rather than logical.[15] (This intuitive element is precisely what the

[14]Swinburne made some of his most notable contributions to this field before his conversion to Orthodoxy in the mid-1990s, and he has made only minor modifications to his approach since that conversion. He has been particularly influential through his trilogy on theism: *The Coherence of Theism* (1977); *The Existence of God* (1979); and *Faith and Reason* (1981)—all published by Oxford: Clarendon. Prominent scholars in this resurgence of the analytical philosophy of religion are, however, mostly Western Christians, among whom William Alston and Alvin Plantinga are as well known as is Swinburne himself. The "analytical philosophy of religion" to which they have contributed seems rooted in an essentially Western conception of theological method.

[15]As the philosopher of religion, John Hick, has put it, the various attempts at evidence for and against God's reality tend to "fall naturally on one side of the balance sheet or the other." Nevertheless, he goes on, we cannot conclude that "one list outweighs the other . . . For it would require us to quantify the values of the different items of evidence . . . [and] any such quantifications could only be arbitrary and subjective" (John Hick, *An Interpretation of Religion: Human Responses to the Transcendent* [London:

Orthodox understanding of the role of the *nous* proclaims.) It is not because atheistic philosophers in this analytic tradition are less able logicians than Swinburne that they come to conclusions very different from his.[16] It is because, as atheists, they experience a greater degree of diminution of this intuitive element.

If Orthodox theology has tended to be wary of discursive "proof" arguments, it does, nevertheless, have a strong sense that a proper reading of the creation points towards the reality and character of its divine Creator. Indeed, it has a particularly strong emphasis on the way in which the created order is transparent to the glory of God. One aspect of this is exhibited in the way in which many patristic writers see nature as exhibiting a unity with spiritual realities in such a way that these realities can be illuminated by what St Gregory of Nyssa speaks of as an ascent: "by way of ascent [lit. '*anagogically*'] we came to know the transcendent nature of the Word from the things that relate to us."[17]

The term *anagogically* is closely related to the more familiar term *allegorically*. According to patristic theology—especially in its Alexandrian component—every passage in Scripture can reveal truths of mystical or moral application through allegorical interpretation. Similarly, in that tradition, aspects of the created cosmos are seen as being readable in a comparable way, with the equivalent of an *allegory* being an *anagogue*. Thus, for example, one of the most common ways of reading nature in this manner

Macmillan, 1989], 123). My disagreement with Hick here is not about his observation that intuitive quantification of "weight" is always implicitly present in proof arguments for the reality of God, but rather about the way in which he has no sense that the enlightenment of the *nous* can prevent this intuitive element from being "arbitrary and subjective."

[16]See, e.g., Michael Martin, *Atheism: A Theological Justification* (Philadelphia: Temple University Press, 1992).

[17]Gregory of Nyssa, *Catechetical Discourse* 2.1. Translation from *Catechetical Discourse: A Handbook for Catechists*, Popular Patristics Series 60, trans. Ignatius Green (Yonkers, NY: St Vladimir's Seminary Press, 2019), 68..

is to see rebirth in nature—Spring after Winter—as an anagogue of the resurrection of the body. Another very common use of this kind of understanding focuses on a group of images concerning light and heat, which are held to indicate something of the nature of God.

This mode of interpretation is not seen by the Fathers as a matter of useful but essentially arbitrary didactic parallels. It represents, in fact, a mode of natural theology. As one commentator has put it, anagogical interpretation represents, for this tradition, "no mere illustration in which heterogeneous objects are placed side by side for comparison." Rather, it is seen as being rooted in "a principle, part of the structure of nature." The creation is understood to be such that it is "possible to argue straight from nature to the spiritual, and then to pass back to nature with new understanding of its significance in this respect."[18]

This does not mean that the patristic writers see natural theology as involving nothing but argument based on the discursive reasoning faculty (*dianoia*). Not only, as we have noted, is there a strong sense that this faculty can only function adequately when based on the spiritual knowledge that arises from the proper use of the intuitive faculty (*nous*), there is also in their work a subtle and somewhat complex attitude towards the embryonic natural theology that was to be found in the philosophy of the ancient Hellenic world. This complexity may be seen especially in the works of the Cappadocian Fathers: Saints Basil the Great, Gregory of Nyssa, and Gregory of Nazianzus. The last of of these was typical of all three in seeing human belief in the existence of "the creative and sustaining cause of all" as consonant with both "sight and the law of nature."[19]

[18]D. S. Wallace-Hadrill, *The Greek Patristic View of Nature* (Manchester, Manchester University Press, 1968), 126.

[19]Gregory of Nazianzus, *Oration* 28.6. Translation from *On God and Christ: The Five Theological Orations and Two Letters to Cledonius*, Popu-

The three Cappadocian Fathers express their use of natural theology in slightly different but complementary ways. St Gregory of Nyssa speaks explicitly about three legitimate sources of theological understanding: the thought of "those who philosophized outside the faith"; the "inspired writings" of the Old and New Testaments; and what he calls "the common apprehension of humanity."[20] St Basil, on the other hand, is less explicit about—and perhaps more cautious towards—the role of secular philosophy, preferring a tripartite taxonomy involving conceptions that are "common," "those that are gathered . . . for us from the Scriptures"; and those which "we have received from the unwritten tradition of the fathers."[21] As a modern commentator has noted, however, such differences of emphasis are not of major significance compared to what unites the Cappadocians, and the implicit natural theology of the Greek philosophical tradition is, for all of them, an authentic source of insight.[22]

Indeed, this commentator, Jaroslav Pelikan, has produced what is perhaps the most extended and useful account of the patristic encounter with the classical tradition of natural theology. He makes a helpful distinction between what he calls "natural theology as apologetics" and "natural theology as presupposition." The former of these categories indicates the need to expound what Gregory of Nyssa calls "the rational basis of our religion" for those who are "seriously searching for the rational basis of the

lar Patristics Series 23, trans. Frederick Williams and Lionel Wickham (Crestwood, NY: St Vladimir's Seminary Press, 2002), 40 (modified).

[20]Gregory of Nyssa, Against Eunomius 1.186 (NPNF[1] 5:53, modified).

[21]Basil the Great, *On the Holy Spirit* 9, 22. Translation from *On the Holy Spirit*, Popular Patristics Series 42, trans. Stephen M. Hildebrand (Yonkers, NY: St Vladimir's Seminary Press, 2011), 52.

[22]Jaroslav Pelikan, *Christianity and Classical Culture: The Metamorphosis of Natural Theology in the Christian Encounter with Hellenism* (New Haven and London: Yale University Press, 1993) 24–5.

mystery."[23] The latter category relates to the way in which—even when apologetic needs are no longer paramount—theology is still inevitably and strongly affected by what a twentieth-century philosopher has called the "fundamental assumptions" of any particular epoch and culture: those notions which "adherents of all the various systems within the epoch unconsciously presuppose . . . [since] no other way of putting things has ever occurred to them."[24] For Pelikan, who quotes this passage as supporting his understanding of the Cappadocians' work, the preconceptions of the classical philosophical tradition are crucial to understanding the way in which aspects of the "doctrinal patrimony to the inheritors of Nicene orthodoxy . . . were rooted in natural theology."[25]

This notion of what is unconsciously presupposed in patristic writings is important because it allows us to read those writings in a more nuanced way than we might otherwise do, and to see the importance of Fr Georges Florovsky's observation that to "follow the Fathers does not mean simply to quote their sentences. It means to acquire their *mind.*"[26]

A good historical example of this need—one that does not involve science as such—relates to the concept of *nature* as it was applied to the christological controversies of the fifth century. The christological *two natures* formula of the Council of Chalcedon—which is central to our Orthodox Tradition—was controversial among Christians at the time of the council for reasons that have only recently become clear. Over the past few decades, talks between Orthodox scholars and those of non-Chalcedonian Eastern Christian communities—who still reject the formula—have

[23]Gregory of Nyssa, *Catechetical Discourse* 15:4 (cf. PPS 60:98).

[24]A. N. Whitehead, *Science and the Modern World* (New York: Mentor Books, 1948) 49f.

[25]Pelikan, *Christianity and Classical Culture*, 185.

[26]Georges Florovsky, "The Ethos of the Orthodox Church," *Ecumenical Review* 12 (1960): 188.

indicated that this rejection is not based on a heretical under-standing. Rather, it is based on the way in which the usual non-Chalcedonian way of understanding the term *nature* is such that (as Peter Bouteneff has noted) "asserting two natures in Christ leads inexorably to positing two hypostases"—a conclusion that would take those who understand the term *nature* in this way onto "untenable ground."[27]

This observation underlines for us that adherence to the *two natures* formula can only be understood as truly Orthodox if the term *nature* is used in a particular, dynamic way.[28] If the term is understood as many of the opponents of the *two natures* formula understood it,[29] then that formula is not a legitimate expression of the Orthodox Tradition.

This issue of how to understand the different formulae produced by the Chalcedonians and their opponents may seem to suggest that the process involved in understanding the mind of the Fathers is simply one of ensuring philosophical exactitude. This perception is certainly partially valid, since—as Bouteneff observes in relation to these formulae—when terminology "is used with care and precision" we find that "the divisions between the formulations dissipate."[30] Even so, we must remember that—while acuity at this level is sometimes of the greatest importance to a full understanding of the writings of the Fathers—what is

[27]See Peter Bouteneff, "Christ and Salvation"; in Mary B. Cunningham and Elizabeth Theokritoff, *The Cambridge Companion to Orthodox Christian Theology* (Cambridge: Cambridge University Press, 2008), 101.

[28]For an accessible brief account of this, see Eugene Webb, *In Search of the Triune God: The Christian Paths of East and West* (Columbia, MO: University of Missouri Press, 2014) 95–96.

[29]See the comments of John S. Romanides, "St Cyril's 'One Physis or Hypostasis of God the Logos Incarnate' and Chalcedon," in Paul R. Fries and Tiran Nersoran, *Christ in East and West* (Macon, GA: Mercer University Press, 1987), 15–34.

[30]Bouteneff, "Christ and Salvation," 101.

meant by having the patristic mind requires something more than having a degree of "care and precision" that can be acquired through the use of the discursive, rational faculty (*dianoia*). What is essential to having the mind of the Fathers is—as many of those Fathers have stressed—an essentially intuitive discernment of divine realities.

Typically, as we have noted, this level of discernment was explained by the Fathers in terms of the *noetic* perception that arises from the liberation of the *nous* from the diminution of its functions in fallen humanity. For the Orthodox Christian understanding, therefore, what is central to the Fathers' mind is not their words, as such, since these can be affirmed in a way that mistakes their intention. Rather, what is central is what we might call the Fathers' *spiritual instinct*: the noetic perception that constituted the foundation on which their verbal constructions were built.

It is in terms of this patristic focus on something deeper than verbal expression that we should, in my view, understand Florovsky's sense of our need, in the present day, to develop a *neo-patristic synthesis*. This perspective will move us beyond the views of those who see this synthesis as requiring little more than explanation of the Fathers' verbal expressions in terms that are readily comprehensible to present day believers. It will take us, instead, towards the views of those who recognize the need, not only to increase comprehensibility in this way, but also to make a clear distinction between what is central to the *mind* of the Fathers and the various ways in which they expressed this "spiritual instinct" in terms of non-theological beliefs that were common in their own time.

Of course, we still find some of these non-theological beliefs helpful to us. Some of them, however—especially the Fathers' scientific beliefs—we may now find unhelpful or even distinctly problematical. This recognition reinforces our sense that the theological wheat of the Fathers' writings needs to be separated from the scientific chaff that was sometimes used in their explanations. This separation will ensure that their scientific inaccuracy does not affect the continuing accessibility of their religious meaning.

This need to understand the Fathers' meaning at a deeper level does not arise only from science, however. It arises also from the historical observation that the Fathers were, in their writings, often responding to particular questions that had arisen within the Christian community of their own time. The forms in which these questions were put inevitably had an influence on the form in which the answers were given, especially when both questions and answers were based on "fundamental assumptions" that we may no longer see as self-evident.[31]

It is in this context that can we can understand the way in which the verbal formulae of the Fathers were often shaped by the way in which they felt the need to employ, not only individual philosophical terms such as *nature*, but also wider philosophical frameworks that were familiar to their audiences, such as Neo-Platonism. These frameworks were, of course, modified in patristic usage so as not to be incompatible with the realities of the Christian revelation. Nevertheless, the use of non-Christian philosophical frameworks inevitably constrained the way in which the

[31]There is sometimes, in our Orthodox community, an unfortunate tendency to downplay or even ignore this fact. As Fr John Behr has perceptively noted, we have often started with what we think we already know and then looked back to the Fathers "simply to find confirmation." This, he argues, carries a great risk of misconstruing what the Fathers were saying since, as he rightly notes, "if the questions being debated are not understood, it will be difficult, if not impossible, to understand the answers." (John Behr, "Faithfulness and Creativity"; in John Behr, Andrew Louth, and Dimitri Conomos, *Abba: The Tradition of Orthodoxy in the West—Festschrift for Bishop Kallistos (Ware) of Diokleia* [Crestwood, NY: St Vladimir's Seminary Press, 2003], 74.)

Fathers' spiritual instinct about that revelation could be expressed verbally. Indeed, it may now cause us to misread what was central to their message because, as Elizabeth Theokritoff has warned, we may wrongly take "their starting point for their conclusion."[32]

These points do not, of course, mean that we should treat the language of the Fathers with anything other than the utmost seriousness. (As Peter Bouteneff has put it, it is "the language of the ecumenical councils, and thus constitutes an enduring and definitive reference point. Furthermore, it is constantly sung in our liturgy, which gives it an ongoing currency in the life of the Church.")[33] What is does mean, however, is that we need not only to examine and be familiar with the Fathers' vocabulary, but to seek for the "inner meaning" that they intended this vocabulary to convey, and where necessary to clarify this meaning in terms of the scientific understandings and philosophical language of our own day. While being careful not to abandon or dilute anything that is central to the patristic understanding, we must use these insights into the nature of any legitimate neo-patristic synthesis both to refine and to deepen our appreciation of that understanding.

[32]Theokritoff makes this remark in the context of a discussion of the Cappadocian Fathers, warning that "the modern reader, to whom their language is alien . . . [may] mistake their Platonic starting point for their conclusion." However, she goes on, this would be to misread their intention in using this language, which is to stress that it is "for the sake of the whole creation that man the microcosm receives the divine inbreathing, so that nothing in creation should be deprived of a share in communion with God." See Elizabeth Theokritoff, "Creator and Creation," in Mary B. Cunningham and Elizabeth Theokritoff, eds., *The Cambridge Companion to Orthodox Christian Theology* (Cambridge: Cambridge University Press, 2008), 65.

[33]Bouteneff, "Christ and Salvation," 102.

chapter four

RATIONALITY IN SCIENCE AND THEOLOGY

The two outstanding philosophers of science of the past century were Karl Popper and Thomas Kuhn. More than half a century after the publication of their main works, the philosophy of science is still, to some extent, based on an attempt to assess their contrasting views and provide an account that incorporates the valid elements of both.

When any particular scientist or group of scientists does a piece of research with interesting results, these results need to be shared with other scientists. The normal way of doing this has, for several generations, been to submit a "paper"—a report of the method and results of that research—to an academic journal devoted to the branch of science to which the research relates.[1]

---

[1]Submission to the journal may well have been preceded by a process of "trying out" the new idea on colleagues in an informal (discussion) or semi-formal (seminar) way, though this will not always be the case, especially if there is a perceived danger of being "scooped" by others. The journal to which the paper is submitted will usually be one specializing in the sub-discipline in which the research will be of most interest, since few journals are devoted to new results in science as a whole, or even to particular sciences like physics. Solid state physicists and astrophysicists, for example, have several journals devoted to their own sub-disciplines, and under normal circumstances those in one sub-discipline will be at best only partially aware of what is published in the journals devoted to the other sub-discipline. Indeed,

The editors of the journal, before deciding whether to publish the submitted paper, will usually send it, without revealing the identity of the author or authors, to one or more experts in the paper's research area. The purpose of this "peer review" is to check that the method is appropriate to the question being asked, that the logic applied to the work is not flawed, and that nothing of significance that might affect the results or conclusions has been ignored. The reviewers may recommend that the paper be accepted or rejected for publication, or may recommend particular changes, after which it will be acceptable.

If the paper is published, its content is then subjected to the criticism of the whole community of scientists in that discipline. This criticism may be implicit, in that the paper may be effectively ignored and rarely if ever be cited in others' work.[2] More importantly, the paper may be challenged. The results—especially if unanticipated—may be repeated to check that they are not the result of some flaw in the instrumentation. The assumptions on which the work is based may be questioned, and even if the observational or experimental results are accepted, the interpretation of those results may be challenged.

This particular process of testing and receiving new work was not exactly the same in the distant past, and may perhaps be modified in future.[3] But the important thing to recognize is that

even in their own journals, time constraints are such that they may well read only those papers that are particularly relevant to their own research.

[2]In scientists' career paths, the "citation index," which measures this use of the paper by others, is a significant factor in whether they are hired or promoted.

[3]The coming into being of scientific journals arose from the need to make more efficient a much older system of correspondence and mutual criticism between leading scientific thinkers. In future, the present system of publication in peer-reviewed journals may change, in that the electronic communications now available—already sometimes making online journals more important than their printed counterparts—may give rise to new forms

the scientific community's activity has been, and will continue to be, based on the assumption that the work of this community is properly one in which numerous people, committed to rational understanding of natural phenomena, evaluate the work of particular individuals or groups of researchers in such a way that at least some of this work—surviving all attempts to perceive its flaws—becomes incorporated into a robust and coherent understanding of the physical world.

The process of this incorporation is a complex one, since different pieces of research will have different relationships with what is already perceived as well-established. Some, as we have noted, make a distinction between the terms *hypothesis* and *theory*, seeing the former as representing little more than a "hunch" that some particular way of looking at things will prove fruitful. Only if this hunch does indeed prove fruitful—in the sense that good evidence is found to back it up—can it deserve, according to this view, to be called a *theory*.[4]

In practice, however, even the term *hypothesis* usually represents more than a hunch, since the hunch on which it is based will, before it is presented to the wider scientific community, be tested to the extent that it may be seen as clearly promising and worthy of further research. (Often, it will be hidden from rivals until it has reached this stage.) Thus it is at least implicitly recognized,

of even more efficient mutual criticism and evaluation. The recent rise of so-called "open access" journals may also weaken the pre-publication process of peer-review, making the informal post-publication review process even more important.

[4]This distinction points to the fact that Darwin's evolutionary perspectives may have begun as no more than a kind of hunch, but by the time that he published his views they were already far more than that, and now—with genetic insights to back up these views—they constitute an extremely robust theory. The common argument among religious fundamentalists that this understanding can be ignored because it is "just a theory" is, quite simply, using the term *theory* wrongly.

within the scientific community, that the degree of robustness of any particular hypothesis or theory needs to be evaluated.

Some theories, because of the wide range of data that seem to support them, become what one philosopher of science, Imre Lakatos, has called *core theories*, which are unlikely to be challenged unless compelling evidence for their inadequacy becomes evident. In relation to these core theories, however, there will inevitably exist what he calls *auxiliary hypotheses*: less well substantiated and sometimes competing theoretical frameworks, which give rise to research programs that attempt to give them a more substantial status than they have at present.[5] In practice, a wide spectrum of degrees of general acceptance of scientific propositions is evident from the way in which researchers treat them.

It should be noted, however, that even if a passion for scientific understanding is their chief motivation, scientists are not simply rational beings. The notion of *competing* research programs—though usually expressed in terms of the testable, rational choices available—points to the fact that different research groups or individuals are often competitive rivals. As such, they display many of the human weaknesses that we associate with rivalry and status-seeking. Scientists are certainly searching for rational understanding, but at the same time (as those close to any scientific community will know) they are often emotionally attached to their own work in a way that combines intellectual judgment with pride and fear that can distort that judgment. Scientists tend to defend their own hypotheses even after most of their peers regard them as having been fatally weakened by the work or criticism of others.[6] They also sometimes denigrate the

5See, e.g., Imre Lakatos, "Falsification and the Methodology of Scientific Research Programmes," in I. Lakatos and A. Musgrave, eds., *Criticism and the Growth of Knowledge* (Cambridge: Cambridge University Press, 1970), 91ff.

6In my own original field of scientific expertise, an excellent example of this is the way in which one of the most brilliant astrophysicists of the

hypotheses of their competitors in a way that goes beyond purely rational criticism.

The process of scientific debate, influenced as it is by distortions arising from status-seeking and rivalry, is undoubtedly one that is susceptible to interesting sociological analysis. It would be wrong, however, to suggest that in most cases sociological factors have more than a short-term effect on scientific progress. However strongly some particular theory is upheld or rejected by even the most influential scientists at any one time, the fact that new results are arising all the time means that, in normal science, if evidence *can* be found indicating that these judgments require modification, then sooner or later it very probably *will* be found. It is for this reason that scientists—even when they acknowledge the sociological factors that affect their community's life—tend to see these factors, not as undermining the scientific enterprise, but simply as slowing it down.[7]

There may, however, be an aspect of the sociology of the scientific community that means that this relatively rapid correcting factor—usually effective over a few years or at most a few decades—is not straightforwardly operative. This is the fact that scientists operate not just with loyalty to a particular research

twentieth century, Fred Hoyle, defended his "steady state" theory of the universe's expansion long after most of his colleagues had judged the evidence for the presently-accepted "Big Bang" theory to have conclusively disproved his proposal.

[7]The acceptance of plate tectonics as a valid understanding of the Earth's continents represents a good example of this process. Beginning in a rather general concept of "continental drift" in the early twentieth century, based on the shapes of the continents, there was rigorous criticism of this hypothesis by eminent scientists such as Harold Jeffreys and Charles Schuchert, and for several decades the notion was widely regarded as untenable. The concept gained acceptance, however, through new insights from such things as paleomagnetism and bathymetry of the deep ocean floor, and over a period of only a few years in the 1960s an "improbable" understanding became a generally accepted one.

program. In addition, they operate with the "core theories" of their discipline. Physicists, for example, are very unlikely to question the notion of conservation of momentum—which is just such a core theory—because it has so much evidence in its favor. Even if they observe a situation in which this conservation seems to be violated, they are far less likely to assume that the core theory has been falsified than to hypothesize the existence of an unobserved particle that carries the "missing" momentum, for which they then begin to search. (Indeed, this kind of momentum disparity led to the discovery of the neutrino.)

There are times, however, when this feature of normal science is interrupted, in that aspects of core theories are questioned, at least by a few. Thomas Kuhn has drawn our attention to those rather rare periods in which a particular scientific problem has proved insoluble for a considerable period, so that what he calls "normal science" begins to break down and a period begins in which previously unquestioned core theories are questioned by at least a minority of researchers. These periods may inaugurate what Kuhn calls *scientific revolutions*—the early twentieth century change from the classical dynamics of Isaac Newton to the relativistic dynamics of Albert Einstein being a key example.[8] What such revolutions make clear, Kuhn argues, is that scientists—who in periods of normal science can easily think of themselves as simply obeying some set of rational rules in deciding between competing theories—are in fact making theory choices in a more subtle and personal way. In Kuhn's analysis, this is related to the fact that their whole education as scientists has initiated them

[8]Physicists nowadays are taught correctly what theoretical speculations led to the theory being proposed, but are often taught incorrectly that certain key experiments were decisive in the immediate acceptance of relativistic theory. In practice, some leading physicists resisted the change for some years after these key experiments, and the process of general acceptance was a complex one.

into what he calls a *paradigm*: not simply a set of formal theories, but a framework of thought and practice inculcated by standard examples of problem solutions in a field.

Such a scientific paradigm, according to Kuhn, involves not only the acceptance of a certain set of theories and practices, but also a certain domain of data that are interpreted in terms of the paradigm, so that there is no independent pool of data that can provide a logical means of choosing between an existing paradigm and a proposed new one. Most scientific activity—what Kuhn calls "normal science"—takes place within a universally-accepted paradigm, so this "theory laden" characteristic of data does not lead to obvious problems, and choice between theories is very largely an uncontroversial matter once the relevant data are available and clear.[9] But the shift of a scientific community from one paradigm to another may be far more problematic and controversial. Such a shift is, as Kuhn points out, a matter of *gestalt*-type conversion, in which the world is seen in a new way. During a revolutionary period, proponents of competing paradigms suffer from what he calls *incommensurability*—an inability not only to agree on the relevance and weight to be accorded to particular data, but even to speak about those data in the same language.

Kuhn's analysis,[10] published in 1962, evoked a heated debate among philosophers of science about the basic rationality of science. Some went further than Kuhn himself and advocated a kind of radical opportunism as far as setting up research programs was concerned.[11] Others, picking up on other aspects of Kuhn's

[9] Even here, however—as another philosopher of science, Michael Polanyi, has argued—theory choice is still not simply a matter of obedience to logical rules, since a kind of "tacit judgment" is also involved. See Michael Polanyi, *Personal Knowledge* (London: Routledge and Kegan Paul, 1958).

[10] Kuhn, *The Structure of Scientific Revolutions*.

[11] See, e.g., Paul Feyerabend, *Against Method*, rev. ed. (London: Verso, 1988).

analysis, used insights from the sociology of knowledge to argue that any particular scientific paradigm is simply a social construction. (This was, in fact, one of the roots of the kind of postmodernist analysis that we shall examine presently.)

The majority of philosophers of science of the present time have, however, reacted to Kuhn's approach, not by attempting to be even more radical, but by attempting to incorporate what are widely seen as his genuine insights into a framework within which a basic scientific rationality can be defended. At the same time, they generally agree that because of the validity of some of Kuhn's insights—into the theory-laden character of data in particular—the attempts to analyze scientific rationality that were common in philosophy until the mid-twentieth century cannot be sustained.

Some scientists, for example, still speak rather loosely about some scientific theory having been *verified,* despite the fact that there has long been a philosophical recognition that scientific theory is always *underdetermined* by data—i.e., that any set of data can in principle be explained by more than one theory.[12]

[12]Usually the Occam's razor principle is used to justify choosing the simplest theory that fits the data, but occasionally this turns out not to be valid. Thus, for example, any competent physicist will recognize that if we had only the data that were available to the scientists of the early nineteenth century, we would have to acknowledge the possibility that either Newton's classical or Einstein's relativistic equations (not then formulated) would adequately "fit" those data. We would have no way of choosing between the two frameworks other than by doing what scientists usually do: to choose (by the Occam's razor principle) the simplest of the possible explanatory theories. And with that particular set of data, this criterion would lead us to choose Newton's theory, which we can now recognize would be the wrong choice, since data now available have been shown to be compatible with Einstein's equations but not with Newton's. Prior to the formulation of relativity theory, people used to speak of Newton's theories as having been "verified" by experiment; but in practice, as is now clear, all that had been shown was that they provided a very good predictive or "puzzle solving" ability over a

More subtly minded scientists now tend to talk about the theories that are well supported by data as *well established* or *robust* ones rather than as verified ones, since the notion of verification had in fact largely been abandoned by philosophers of science even before Kuhn's analysis appeared.[13]

This was not only because of acknowledgment that theories are underdetermined by data but also because of the radical rethinking of the nature of scientific activity presented by Karl Popper (originally published in German in 1934 but only widely discussed internationally after its publication in English in 1959, not long before Kuhn's analysis appeared.)[14] If scientists aren't, strictly speaking, *verifying* theories, Popper had asked himself, then what are they doing? The answer he gave was based on his observation that the search for new scientific theories usually arises from new data that do not seem to fit accepted theories, and thus, as he put it, *falsify* those theories. He pointed out that a new theory, to be acceptable, has to explain both the old data, which do not challenge the old theory, and the new data, which do. While Popper shared the conviction of those who spoke about verification that science is a logical activity, he in effect turned their program on its head by locating the essential feature of scientific activity in criticism rather than justification, and substituting

particular range conditions: essentially that in which no velocities comparable with that of light are involved.

[13]The notion of scientific "verification" of theory, especially as embodied in the kind of *logical positivism* advocated by people like A. J. Ayer, was still in the mid-twentieth century extremely influential among both philosophers and the general public, and among the latter it is still often assumed at a quasi-instinctive level.

[14]Karl Popper, *The Logic of Scientific Discovery* (London: Hutchison, 1959). For much of the rest of the twentieth century, philosophers of science often saw their task in part in terms of a kind of Popper versus Kuhn debate. Whichever side they tended to support, however, it was widely agreed that the old concept of verification was defunct.

theory for observation, and fallibilism for certainty or probability. *Falsifiability*, in this view, became the touchstone for whether or not a statement could be regarded as scientific.

Since Popper's thesis became widely known, many have recognized its oversimplifications, both in terms of the way in which Kuhn's notion of the theory-laden character of data needs to be taken into account and in terms of Lakatos's distinction between core theories and auxiliary hypotheses. In addition, Popper himself, in his later publications, expanded his views in a way that made it clear that he did not believe falsifiability to be a simple criterion for rationality. Many working scientists, however, even if they are philosophically sophisticated enough to have moved beyond the sort of verificationism that Popper made redundant, now adopt a stance that is essentially a Popperian one in an oversimplified form. Moreover, they often fail to limit themselves to what is intrinsic to the Popperian approach, adopting a kind of scientism which, as we have noted, makes inadequate assumptions about the limits of the scientific method.

Those who manifest this kind of scientism often express their views in terms of the way in which theology should be seen as irrational because it arises from data that are not repeatable and publicly available in the way that scientific data are. The most sophisticated philosophical attempt to sustain a view of this kind was that of the *logical positivists* who, around the middle of the twentieth century, were highly influential, not only within the philosophical community but also beyond it because of the propagation of their views in widely read books such as A J. Ayer's *Language, Truth and Logic*.[15]

By the time that Ayer was writing, however, the logical positivists were already under attack from many of their philosophical colleagues, on the grounds that their stress on verifiability was

---

[15]A. J. Ayer, *Language, Truth and Logic* (London: Gollancz, 1946).

incoherent, being based on assumptions that were not themselves verifiable.[16] It was, however, not primarily this critique that led to the complete downfall of this approach only a few years later. The *coup de grâce* came with the revolution in the philosophy of science that we have examined, inaugurated by the work of Popper and Kuhn. Philosophical defenders of the rationality of science now recognize that they require a far more subtle approach to the notion of rationality than was once common among them, and their philosophical explorations of this notion only rarely now use the sciences as the main model of rational human activity.

Scientists themselves are rarely sophisticated at a philosophical level, however, and a small but vociferous minority of them still seem to be attached to a kind of scientism that is not intrinsic to the pursuit of science. As has sometimes been pointed out, the argument put forward by this minority is analogous to the argument that fish with a width of less than some particular value cannot exist because they have never been caught in a particular net, which happens to have a mesh size exactly that of the smallest fish that they believe can be caught. The point here is that the possibility of the existence of methodological nets with a finer mesh than science—which can, so to speak, catch smaller fish—is simply dismissed by the advocates of scientism as nonsense.[17]

---

[16]One such assumption, for example, was that the past is a reliable guide to the future. As Bertrand Russell pointed out, however, the chicken that has been fed every day of its life will be surprised when, on Christmas Eve, instead of being fed, it has its head chopped off in preparation for the Christmas feast.

[17]That this dismissal is questionable even before we take theology into account is evident from the fact that this kind of scientism often regards as dubious or even meaningless a number of disciplines that most atheists can recognize have have a good claim to rationality. For some of the advocates of scientism, even the social sciences—the methodologies and conceptual schemes of which constitute a different kind of "net" to their own—are often regarded with grave suspicion. Philip Clayton has formulated an interesting

A particular version of scientism, which has received much publicity in the early years of the twenty-first century, is that associated with the so-called *new atheism* popularized by the biologist, Richard Dawkins.[18] There is often, in the writings of Dawkins and his supporters, a kind of ill-informed contempt for any kind of philosophy that does not correspond straightforwardly to what they see as scientific "common sense."[19] Indeed, their lack of philosophical sophistication in this respect is one of the reasons that the philosopher Michael Ruse—himself an atheist—has commented that Dawkins makes him "ashamed to be an atheist."[20]

Moreover, among many of the new atheists, assertions about the irrational nature of theology are based, not only on a philosophically outmoded scientism, but on a rather striking ignorance of what theology actually is. The element of rational reflection

argument that the social sciences form a bridge that links the rationality of physics—the "hardest" of the sciences—with that of theology; see Philip Clayton, *Explanation from Physics to Theology: An Essay in Rationality and Religion* (New Haven: Yale University Press, 1989).

[18]Dawkins's abilities as a popularizer of science are, it must be said, outstanding, and in my own view his anti-religious polemic, though in some respects ridiculous, is based on an attitude of passion for truth that is more praiseworthy than many of his opponents are able to recognize. See the comments in Christopher C. Knight, *The God of Nature: Incarnation and Contemporary Science* (Minneapolis: Fortress, 2007), 10–21.

[19]This kind of reliance on "common sense" to defend atheism is perhaps one of the reasons that biologists seem to be more outspoken in that defense than are physicists. The latter, through the development of relativity and quantum mechanics in the twentieth century, are aware that aspects of the world can seem counter-intuitive, and are therefore aware that "common sense" is not always a reliable guide. They sometimes joke among themselves that twenty-first century biologists are still stuck, in this respect, in the nineteenth century.

[20]*http://www.beliefnet.com/columnists/scienceandthesacred/2009/08/ why-i-think-the-new-atheists-are-a-bloody-disaster.html.* For his own more balanced approach, see Michael Ruse, *Atheism: What Everyone Needs to Know* (Oxford: Oxford University Press, 2015).

in theology—characteristic of both the patristic literature and of much recent theological exploration—is simply not recognized by them. Instead, a caricature—based on the notion of the religious believer's "blind faith"—is frequently substituted for the reality.

There is, of course, a sense in which the new atheists are not completely wrong in their focus on the nature of religious faith, since—as they rightly observe—this faith is not based on the kind of "sight" that their scientism insists is the only kind that can exist. Christians do assert that there exists a basic historical revelation of God to which the believer has responded at a level deeper than that of simple discursive rationality. We should, however, resist the temptation to speak about "blind" faith, not only because Christian faith is—as we have noted in our exploration of Orthodox natural theology—intimately connected to the spiritual "sight" associated with the functioning of the *nous*. We should resist the temptation also because most Christians see their faith (as did the patristic writers) as providing a cohesive understanding of the world.

As we have noted in our exploration of the concept of natural theology, early Christian thinkers saw our created human faculties as being at least potentially fully integrated into our experience of faith, and indeed they sometimes explored the question of how we can know anything—the question of what philosophers call *epistemology*—in an extremely sophisticated way. And while participants in the Western science-theology dialogue have often been more naïve than the patristic writers were in relation to epistemological questions, their fundamental views about the relationship between faith and reason are in some respects not dissimilar to these patristic ones.

An aspect of how this kind of understanding may be expressed by us now arises from an examination of the way in which our religious beliefs would not have a long-term hold on us unless they provided what Kuhn (in the scientific context) has called *puzzle solutions*: ways of making sense of those aspects of our experience that pose questions for our understanding. This is not to say that the theological puzzle-solutions that we find insightful have precisely the same characteristics as the theories that constitute scientific puzzle solutions. Rather, it is to point to the way in which theological understanding gives solutions to *existential* puzzles that arise from our intrinsic need to ask, not only *how* things are, but also *why*.

The point here is that as human beings we naturally ask questions about both mechanism, with which science deals, and about purpose, with which science cannot deal. Our predisposition to ask questions about purpose is not, as some of the new atheists have claimed, simply a matter of culture (although clearly culture may tend either to reinforce or to undermine it). Rather, as recent scientific research has indicated, our tendency to see purpose in the world—the tendency at the heart of our propensity to ask *why* questions—is "hard-wired" into our brains.[21]

The fact of this hard-wiring in itself proves nothing, of course, other than the incorrectness of those new atheists who see religious belief as nothing more than cultural conditioning. It is, however, certainly very suggestive for the theologian who affirms the importance of the kind of Orthodox natural theology that we

---

[21]Justin L. Barrett, *Why Would Anyone Believe in* God (Lanham: Altamira, 2004), and Justin L. Barrett, *Born Believers: The Science of Children's Religious Beliefs* (London: Simon and Schuster, 2012), are both based on experimental cognitive science. Despite these studies' parallels with those of the atheist Pascal Boyer, Barrett has been widely accused by the new atheists of having a religious agenda in his scientific studies, simply because he himself is a religious believer. He does not argue, however, that religious belief is correct (though his insights are compatible with that belief). Rather, he has demonstrated convincingly that views commonly held by the new atheists—that childhood religious belief is the result either of indoctrination or of "evolved gullibility"—are untenable from a scientific perspective.

have examined, which is based on the notion of the existence of a human faculty—the *nous*—through which God may be known at an intuitive level.

Moreover, even before this kind of natural theology is taken into account, we can surely see significance in the fact that the religious solutions that Christians believe are available in answer to our "why" questions often exhibit the four main characteristics of modern scientific theory as described by Ian Barbour. These, as they apply to science, have been summarized by him as follows:

1. Agreement with Data. This is the most important criterion, though it never provides proof that a theory is true, for other theories not yet developed may fit the data as well or better. Theories are always underdetermined by data. Nor does disagreement with data prove a theory false, since ad hoc modifications or unexplained anomalies can be tolerated for an indefinite period. But agreement with data and predictive success—especially the prediction of novel phenomena not previously anticipated—constitute impressive support for a theory.

2. Coherence. A theory should be consistent with other accepted theories and, if possible, conceptually interconnected with them. Scientists also value the internal coherence and simplicity of a theory (simplicity of formal structure, smallest number of independent or ad hoc assumptions, aesthetic elegance, transformational symmetry, and so forth).

3. Scope. Theories can be judged by their comprehensiveness or generality. A theory is valued if it unifies previously disparate domains, if it is supported by a variety of kinds of

evidence, or if it is applicable to wide ranges of the relevant variables.

4. Fertility. A theory is evaluated not just by its past accomplishments but by its current ability and future promise in providing a framework for an ongoing research program. Is the theory fruitful in encouraging further theoretical elaboration, in generating new hypotheses, and in suggesting new experiments? Attention is directed here to the continuing research activity of a scientific community rather than to the finished product of their work.[22]

Barbour goes on to explain how each of these characteristics of the development of scientific theory has its equivalent in the development of theological doctrine, albeit with significant differences of emphasis.[23] A major difference between scientific and religious activities that Barbour points out is the importance of religious experience to the theological task, especially in relation to the stories and rituals that define any religious community. He acknowledges that interpretation of such experience can never simply be the product of logical reasoning from data. It results, in addition, from what he calls "acts of the creative imagination" in which analogies and models are prominent. He points out, however, that analogies and models have an important part to play,

---

[22]Ian G. Barbour, *Religion in an Age of Science: The Gifford Lectures 1989–1991* (London: SCM, 1990), 1:34.

[23]Barbour does, admittedly, make these comparisons in a way that tends to underestimate differences between different religious traditions, and to talk about "science" and "religion" as though these always incorporated certain well-defined methodologies and boundaries—an assumption that been intelligently questioned from the historian's perspective by Peter Harrison (Peter Harrison, *The Territories of Science and Religion* [Chicago: University of Chicago Press, 2015]). Nevertheless, Barbour's views remain useful, even though the kind of critique that Harrison has offered needs always to be borne in mind.

not only in theology, but also in science. He observes that in scientific activity an analogy is sometimes systematically developed as a conceptual model of a postulated entity that cannot be directly observed, leading to the formulation of a generalized and abstract theory. In a comparable way, he argues, theological models are "drawn from the stories of a tradition and express the structural elements that recur in dynamic form in narratives. These models, in turn, lead to abstract concepts and articulated beliefs that are systematically formalized as theological doctrines."[24]

There are, from an Orthodox perspective, gaps in Barbour's understanding of the parallels and differences between the activities of scientists and theologians. In particular, the Orthodox notion of the role of the *nous* is completely absent from his understanding. He argues convincingly, nevertheless, that there are many parallels between scientific and theological development (at least in the Christian context, which he takes as paradigmatic). These include "the interaction of data and theory (or experience and interpretation); the historical character of the interpretive community; the use of models; and the influence of paradigms or programs." In both fields, Barbour goes on, "there are no proofs, but there can be good reasons for the judgments rendered by the paradigm community." He recognizes what he calls "polarities" in which science and religion put different emphases on one or other of the poles: "objectivity and subjectivity; rationality and personal judgment; universality and historical conditioning; criticism and tradition; and tentativeness and commitment." He stresses, however, that these, on examination, may be seen as "differences of emphasis or degree rather than the absolute contrasts sometimes imagined." The real differences between the two activities, he suggests, lie not in these areas but in those features of religion that are without parallel in science: "the role of story and ritual; the

---

[24]Barbour, *Religion in an Age of Science*, 36.

noncognitive functions of religious models in evoking attitudes and encouraging personal transformation; the type of personal involvement characteristic of religious faith; and the idea of revelation in historical events."[25]

Such differences (which the Orthodox Christian will certainly affirm) do not, however, affect Barbour's basic point: that in developing a theology appropriate to their community's experience, Christian believers (or at any rate the systematic theologians among them) are not simply acting on "blind faith" but are using their rational faculties in a way that is appropriate to the subject of their investigation.

[25]Barbour, *Religion in an Age of Science*, 65.

chapter five

REALISM IN SCIENCE
AND THEOLOGY

S cientists, when they talk about entities such as quarks—
which they cannot observe directly but can only infer
through theoretical exploration of experimental results—
usually believe that these entities really exist. Religious believers—when they speak about the God whom they cannot observe
directly—are in a comparable way also *realists* in their beliefs.

As people of faith, we Orthodox may not feel the need to question this latter assumption, but as people interested in Christian
apologetics we do need to do so. We cannot, therefore, ignore
the questions of whether scientific and theological forms of realism can be defended philosophically and of what the connection
between them might be. When we examine these questions it turns
out that, just as it is wrong to assume that scientific rationality and
theological rationality have no points of contact, so it is also wrong
to assume that scientific and theological realism are unconnected.
Moreover, as we shall see in this chapter, there are resources within
the Orthodox Tradition that are particularly relevant to the question of how realism is to be understood in both fields.

Philosophers use the term *ontology* to describe the concept of
what *really* is, and recognize that not all things to which we refer
have a straightforward ontological status. We can all recognize,

for example, that there is not some essence of "rainbowness" that explains the phenomenon to which we refer when we say to someone "Look, there's a rainbow." When we point to a region of the sky and say this to others standing near us, they can see what we see and understand exactly what we mean, and in this sense the rainbow is certainly real rather than imaginary; our *reference* to it is valid. We recognize, however, that the reference is not to something with a straightforward ontology. What seems to be an "object" is in fact the result of refraction and internal reflection effects when sunlight illuminates small water droplets in the lower atmosphere, and the rainbow's apparent position in space is not exactly the same for all its observers. (If we approach where it seems to be, its apparent position recedes.)

When philosophers and scientists in the Popperian tradition talk about "increasing verisimilitude" in the development of scientific theory, what they are claiming is not only that reference is being made in this "pointing" sense. Nor are they saying only that successive scientific theories make better and better predictions about the world, supplying what Kuhn calls increasingly comprehensive puzzle solutions. In a way that arguably oversimplifies what Popper himself claimed, they are, over and above these claims, usually presuming that scientific theory truly points to what the world consists of—to its ontology—and that successive theories do so ever more accurately. This claim is made not only about what is directly observable but also about entities postulated in scientific theory, such as quarks, which are not directly observable but which—through the theories which speak about them—seem to make sense of what is observable.[1]

[1]Theological talk is at one level of a similar kind, since God cannot be observed directly but can be known in part as a kind of explanation of experience. Theologians rightly stress, however, that talk about God is different in certain important respects from talk of the unobservable entities of scientific theory. God, they emphasize, is not to be understood simply as a thing among

In taking this stance, those in the Popperian tradition are upholding a particular form of *realism* (as opposed to the kind of *instrumentalism* which asserts that scientific theories should not be seen as anything other than a kind of useful fiction that enables us to make accurate predictions about directly observable events). Those who uphold this modern kind of scientific realism often call it *critical realism* because they recognize, with Popper, that scientific theories change over time, and that therefore it is not possible to claim (as would upholders of *naïve realism*) that there is an *exact* correspondence between the entities postulated by some current theory and the ontology of the world.

A dominant strand of the Western science-theology dialogue of recent decades has been based on broad agreement with this realist understanding of the entities spoken of in scientific theory. Yet there are a number of problems associated with this approach that have been debated by philosophers but largely ignored by the dialogue's participants. One of these problems is that scientific theory changes sometimes involve major changes in ontological description, which are hard to see as consonant with the notion of increasing ontological verisimilitude. Moreover, in two successive changes there may not even be a continuous direction of change. As Kuhn himself notes, "Newton's mechanics improves on Aristotle's and . . . Einstein's improves on Newton's as instruments for puzzle-solving." However, he goes on, these successive theories manifest "no coherent direction in their ontological development. On the contrary, in some important respects, though by no means in all, Einstein's general theory of relativity is closer to Aristotle's than either of them is to Newton's."[2]

---

things or a cause among causes, nor is the reality of God simply an abstract hypothesis about the world that may be explored scientifically.

[2]Kuhn, *The Structure of Scientific Revolutions*, 206–7.

Kuhn, on the basis of this and other considerations, took up an essentially anti-realist stance in his understanding of scientific language. This stance has not, however, been widely accepted among philosophers of science. Most working scientists feel instinctively that their theories genuinely point to the way the world really is, and the majority of philosophers would agree that, unless this were the case, the extraordinary success of the sciences—practical as well as theoretical—would be inexplicable.[3]

Some of these philosophers have, however, suggested that a coherent scientific realism should cease focusing on the ontology of entities. Mary Hesse, for example, in her understanding of physics, has argued for what she calls *structural realism*. It is, she says, "undeniable that mathematical structures become ever more unified and universal with every advance in theory; the structural realm of physics is truly progressive." But, she observes, "the substantial description of what the structures relate changes radically from theory to theory."[4] We should, she suggests, be realists about the structures that science claims to reveal, but not about the ontology that is assumed in the description and investigation of these structures.[5]

---

[3]There are, however, exceptions to this generalization; see, e.g., Bas C. van Frasasen, *The Scientific Image* (Oxford: Oxford University Press, 1980), ch. 5.

[4]M. B. Hesse, "Physics, Philosophy and Myth," in R. J. Russell, W. R. Stoeger, and G. V. Coyne, eds., *Physics, Philosophy and Theology: A Common Quest for Understanding* (Vatican City State: Vatican Observatory, 1988), 188.

[5]The "structural realism" that Hesse defends arises from her sense of the way in which the ontology assumed in any theory in physics, while necessary to connect the mathematical structure with empirical observation and experiment, is essentially an interpretation of the theory. Without an assumed ontology, theory development could not take place, but as far as philosophical questions about ontology are concerned, these "substantial" descriptions are secondary. As pictures of the ontology of the world they are

A comparable understanding arises from the work of Rom Harré on what he calls *referential realism*, in which two modes of scientific reference are distinguished. The first—as in the statement "this grey powder is a sample of gallium"—requires, as he puts it, simply the ability to "pick out a figure from a ground." The second—as in the statement "whatever is the cause of these bubbles is a neutrino"—involves the cognitive act of conceiving and accepting a theoretical account of the possible causes of an observed phenomenon.[6] The importance of this distinction, he suggests, is that the latter mode of reference—which he sees as just as truly referential as the former—is in practice often uncritically translated by scientists into the first kind of referential statement through an essentially arbitrary ontological assumption. He gives the example of the neutrino and the cloud chamber bubbles that first revealed its existence. There is, he argues, nothing in the formal referential statement—"whatever is the cause of these bubbles is a neutrino"—that makes it necessary to conceive the neutrino as it is usually conceived: as a particle. (Indeed, he notes, there exists an alternative metaphysics in the understanding advocated by the quantum physicist, David Bohm.[7]) "The logical grammar of the . . . referential format" Harré argues, "is neutral. It is the conservative metaphysical predilections of physicists that push the ontology that way."[8]

Philosophical arguments of this kind—for some reinforced by the notion of "ontological relativity" developed by W. V.

susceptible—unlike the mathematical relationships themselves—to complete change or abandonment.

[6]Rom Harré, *Varieties of Realism: A Rationale for the Natural Sciences* (Oxford: Basil Blackwell, 1986), 101ff.

[7]Harré, *Varieties of Realism*, 316, referring to the approach set out in popular form in David Bohm, *Wholeness and the Implicate Order* (London: Routledge and Kegan Paul, 1980).

[8]Harré, *Varieties of Realism*, 316.

Quine[9]—suggest that we should be wary of accepting the ontologically-focused kind of critical realism that many speak of as a proper interpretation of the status of scientific theory. This justifiable wariness, however, should not be taken to imply that it is not possible to defend the referential success of scientific theory. Rather, it suggests that a kind of radically modified critical realism might be the best way forward in the debate about the nature of scientific understanding.

According to this modified understanding, we can validly explore the structure of the world and *refer* to certain things within that world, but at the same time we must be extremely wary of thinking that we understand what these things are in themselves. Hesse's and Harré's arguments do not mean that there is no ontological basis to the entities referred to in scientific language. What they do indicate, however, is that there may be insurmountable epistemological limitations to our grasp of their ontology.

Many participants in the Western science-theology dialogue—following Barbour's notion of the parallels between theological and scientific rationality—have seen scientific critical realism as having implications for how we should understand the realism of theological language. (Indeed, they often base their understanding of the development of doctrine on it.) But they rarely acknowledge the kind of modification to scientific critical realism that the work of Hesse and Harré suggests is necessary. They therefore fail to see how this modification, if applied to theological as well as to scientific language, may be important in reinforcing the view of theological language that is characteristic of Orthodoxy.

Particularly in the form of it expounded by people like Vladimir Lossky,[10] this Orthodox view of theological language

---

[9]W. V. Quine, "Ontological Relativity," in *Ontological Relativity and Other Essays* (New York: Columbia University Press) 26–68.

[10]Lossky, *Mystical Theology*. We should perhaps note that while Lossky's

manifests an understanding different from any to be found in Western theological traditions. This view is rooted in a number of patristic writings, and especially in those of the Cappadocian Fathers and those attributed to Dionysius the Areopagite. These writings distinguish two possible theological ways: that of *cataphatic* or positive theology, which proceeds by affirmations, and that of *apophatic* or negative theology, which proceeds by negations. Lossky notes that in Western theology these two ways—if acknowledged at all—tend in practice to be reduced to one, simply making negative theology a corrective to affirmative theology. The Orthodox understanding, he suggests, tends to have a different and more radical understanding of the importance of apophaticism, so that cataphatic affirmations are seen primarily as providing a kind of ladder towards an increasingly contemplative and non-conceptual knowledge of God.[11]

Sometimes, the radical apophaticism of Orthodox theological writers is expressed by them only in terms of the Areopagitic recognition that we cannot straightforwardly apply to God categories comprehended in relation to created things. Yet in the patristic period, apophaticism was sometimes understood more broadly. For St Basil the Great, in particular, it was—as Lossky notes—"not the divine essence alone but also created essences that could not be expressed in concepts. In contemplating any object we analyze its properties; it is this which enables us to form concepts. But this analysis can in no case exhaust the content of

interpretation has been a major influence in Orthodox theology over the last two or three generations, this influence has not been uniform. Within the Orthodox component of the science-theology dialogue, for example, Alexei Nesteruk seems to work with a less radical apophaticism than that advocated by Lossky and used in my own work. More generally, we should note that Lossky's perspectives have perhaps been more influential in the Slav strand of Orthodoxy than in the Greek.

[11]Lossky, *Mystical Theology*, 40.

the object of perception." There will always, he goes on, remain a kind of "residue, which escapes analysis and which cannot be expressed in concepts, it is the unknowable depth of things, that which constitutes their true, indefinable essence."[12]

Over and above the modern philosophical arguments about the ontology of created things that I have outlined, this Basilian application of apophaticism to those things may well make Orthodox Christians wary of the simplistic critical realism that is characteristic of the Western science-theology dialogue. They will tend, by contrast, to stress that there are aspects of both God and of created things that are unknowable by us, and adopt what we might call *apophatic critical realism* in relation to both science and theology. Moreover, as we shall see in the next chapter, a further source of wariness for the Orthodox is that most of that dialogue's participants, in their view of critical realism, implicitly assume the kind of materialism that denies the validity of any kind of *idealism*, in which mind is given priority over matter. By contrast, the fact that a kind of idealism is to be found in the patristic literature—and particularly (as we shall see) in the work of St Gregory of Nyssa—will not seem irrelevant to Orthodox when they examine this kind of materialism.

Before exploring that issue, however, we should perhaps note another facet of the Orthodox understanding of language usage that is relevant here: that which—like the thinking of Yves Congar in the West[13]—stresses that what we can know about God does

[12]Lossky, *Mystical Theology*, 33.

[13]Congar stresses that God is known through what he calls "signs" that are always oriented primarily towards salvation, being "proportionate to the human condition" and couched "in the language of men, in images, concepts and judgments like our own" (quoted in W. Henn, "The Hierarchy of Truths According to Yves Congar, O.P.," *Analecta Gregoriana* 246 [1987]: 115). Congar sees the content of these signs as having a genuine ontological content but this must, he insists, be expressed in terms of "mysteries"—partially hidden truths—made present most fully in the liturgical celebration of salva-

not constitute objective knowledge of an abstract kind. Rather, it is to be understood in soteriological terms related to our human condition. Essentially it is *saving* knowledge. Lossky, for example, quite explicitly sees the terms that we apply to God in cataphatic theology as something other than "rational notions which we formulate, the concepts with which our intellect constructs a positive science of the divine nature." Rather, he says, they are "images or ideas intended to guide us and fit our faculties for the contemplation of that which passes all understanding."[14]

Here, an important factor that may help clarify this stress on the human condition is the fact that a comparable focus arises from the way in which philosophers now often suggest that the best way forward in understanding science may be to focus primarily, not on scientific theories, viewed simply as an intellectual framework, but on those who develop this framework.

Within the Western science-theology dialogue, this kind of understanding has, admittedly, been acknowledged by relatively few. A significant exploration of one aspect of it has, however, been begun by Wentzel van Huyssteen in terms of what he calls *postfoundationalism.*[15] This exploration arises from the way in

tion and always, when expressed linguistically, to be approached apophatically. There appears to be much in this approach that echoes understandings found among Orthodox writers.

[14]Lossky, *Mystical Theology*, 40. This focus on theological language as providing a contemplative ladder towards a non-conceptual knowledge of God is comparable to that to be found in the work of another Orthodox writer, Philip Sherrard, who has stressed the way in which God's revelation of himself is both oriented towards and limited by our human condition. See Philip Sherrard, *Christianity: Lineaments of a Sacred Tradition* (Edinburgh: T & T Clarke, 1998), ch. 3.

[15]For a short account of his perspectives, see J. Wentzel van Huyssteen, "Postfoundationalism in Theology and Science," in N. H. Gregersen and J. W. van Huyssteen, eds., *Rethinking Theology and Science: Six Models for the Current Dialogue* (Grand Rapids: Eerdmans, 1998), 13–49.

which a great deal of current philosophical debate takes place in the context of what is often described as *postmodernism* (the metaphysics of which has been explored in a profound way by the Orthodox writer, Christos Yannaras).[16]

This term *postmodernism* is, admittedly, a rather broad umbrella, one that makes exact definition difficult. It can certainly be said, however, that one of the characteristics of postmodernist analysis is a tendency—based in part on the sociological factors that we have glanced at in relation to science—to view all theories, including scientific ones, not so much in terms of reference to the real world as in terms of social construction.

Here, we should note, some postmodernist assessments of science seem—to many philosophers as well as to almost all working scientists—to be remarkably inaccurate. But even if we agree (as we surely should) with much of this critical assessment,[17] this need not entail a rejection of all postmodernist attempts to understand science in terms of social construction. For one of the very positive things that has come out of the climate of thought that postmodernism has fostered is the notion that, rather than focus on abstract notions of rationality and truth in scientific activity, it might be more fruitful to focus on scientists as *rational*

[16]Christos Yannaras, *Postmodern Metaphysics* (Brookline, MA: Holy Cross Orthodox Press, 2004).

[17]One of the most prominent postmodernist analyses of science is that of J. F. Lyotard, and my own criticism of this analysis is broadly consonant with that given by Steven Connor in his *Postmodernist Culture: An Introduction to Theories of the Contemporary* (Oxford: Basil Blackwell, 1989). Connor notes—correctly in my view—that Lyotard "paints a picture of the dissolution of the sciences into a frenzy of relativism in which the only aim is to bound gleefully out of the confinement of musty old paradigms and to trample operational procedures underfoot in the quest for exotic forms of illogic. But this is simply not the case. If some forms of the pure sciences . . . are concerned with the exploration of different structures of thought for understanding reality, then this still remains bound, by and large, to models of rationality, consensus, and correspondence to demonstrable truths" (p. 35).

agents: people whose rational reflection is influenced—and even to some extent conditioned—by the sociological and biological frameworks within which they operate. This does not mean that we must cease to speak of science as a rational activity, but it does mean that we should, as van Huyssteen stresses, see human rationality and the "reality" that it perceives in a broader perspective than has often been the case.[18]

Side by side with this essentially philosophical investigation, there are other factors that provide ways of thinking about the complexity of what it is to be a rational agent. Two of the most important of these are related to the ways in which cognitive scientists are becoming increasingly aware that our mental functions cannot be fully understood properly without considering both our evolutionary history[19] and our embodied character.[20]

---

[18]In pointing this out, Wentzel van Huyssteen has performed a service to the participants in the science-theology dialogue that deserves wider recognition than many of those participants seem to recognize; see J. Wentzel van Huyssteen, "Postfoundationalism in Theology and Science," 13–49.

[19]An understanding of the importance of our evolutionary history for our mental functioning forms the basis of the recently developed discipline of *evolutionary psychology*. Despite the fact that many of the supposed "insights" offered by scholars within this discipline are highly speculative, and likely to undergo considerable modification in the future, the basic insight on which these speculations are based—that certain of our psychological characteristics have emerged in the evolutionary process because they aided survival—seems basically sound from a scientific perspective. Moreover, it is not one that need be questioned from a theological perspective in the context of an understanding of the kind set out in this book, in which (as we shall see) certain outcomes of the evolutionary process are broadly predictable, and so may be seen as in accordance with the will of God. Because of this, the Christian can expect that as the field matures it will offer significant insights into some of the roots of human mental functioning.

[20]It has been increasingly recognized by scientists that human cognition and reflection takes place, not in minds that are unaffected by bodies, but in beings whose mental abilities are embodied—that is, rooted in, and conditioned by, the particular biological form that we have. Part of this insight

The latter insight, about embodiment, is of particular theological importance. It is an insight that arises, scientifically, primarily from results emerging from brain-scanning techniques and from analysis of the effects of brain damage. Because of these results, it is now clear that our cognitive and reflective processes are correlated with, and influenced by, the states of the brain, of other parts of the body, and perhaps of the wider environment in which humans exist. This does not only have implications for our understanding of human rationality and language usage; it is of importance also—as we shall see in the next chapter—for understanding something that is central to our Christian understanding of what it is to be human: what it means to talk about the *soul*.

comes from the detailed experimental results that have led to the increasing sophistication of the notion of embodied cognition now widely held among cognitive scientists.

chapter six

THE HUMAN MIND
AND THE MIND OF GOD

Given the connection between the human mind and what Christians have traditionally called the *soul*, current scientific insights into the embodied character of human mental functioning inevitably raise questions about the reality of this soul. Here, as a preliminary consideration, it is important to recognize that much of what often passes for a Christian understanding of the soul is not based on a specifically Christian anthropology. When true to its biblical and patristic roots, this anthropology has always stressed the essential unity of the human person, expressed in terms of the union of body and soul, or of body, mind, and spirit. All too often, however, Christians have spoken of the soul in a way that is based, not on this unity, but on an ancient Greek kind of matter-denigrating *dualism*, of the kind that for some was reinforced in early modern times by the philosophy of Descartes.

What contemporary science does, by uncovering something of the embodied mechanism of mental functioning, is to challenge any simplistic dualistic view of this kind. We are forced to take with due seriousness the kind of biblical and patristic understanding in which the physical, mental, and spiritual aspects of human beings are seen as components of a created unity, rather than as different entities in some kind of temporary alliance. It is this unity that is proclaimed when we insist that in the world to come we shall not be disembodied souls but will have resurrection bodies.

The kinds of question raised by modern science about the status of the human mind are, in this respect, extremely helpful in our reappropriation of the ancient Christian understanding of the resurrection of the body. There are, however, questions related to our understanding of the unity of the human person in this life that now arise in a new way. Scientific insights—especially those that arise from brain scanning data—indicate the ways in which human mental activity and brain states are correlated. In terms of the scientific methodology that seeks explanation of systems in terms of the component parts of those systems, this inevitably raises the question of whether human mental functioning is nothing more than a kind of secondary phenomenon brought on by electrical and chemical processes in the brain.

This question is, in fact, a special case of a more general question: that of whether reality is ultimately to be understood entirely in terms of the "basic" physical components of the universe, so that all other perceived realities are nothing but *epiphenomena* that have no ultimate reality. At least a few scientists have certainly spoken in this way, and seem to believe that everything that occurs in the cosmos is susceptible to *reduction* to the properties of the universe's basic constituents. In principle, they believe, we could develop a fully-explanatory "theory of everything" that consists of nothing more than a mathematical description of atoms and molecules (or of the more basic entities of which they are constructed).

In speaking in this way, these scientists have fallen into a temptation that sometimes seems to assail certain members of their profession: to stray beyond the legitimate boundaries of their discipline into questions that belong properly to a discipline in which they usually have no training and little insight: that of philosophy. What these people do is to extrapolate, in an unjustifiable manner, from the legitimate way in which the methodology of the sciences usually involves trying to understand systems in terms of the properties of their component parts. They go on to assume or claim, without philosophical justification, that the remarkable success of this *methodological reductionism* entails that we should accept the kind of *ontological reductionism* in which reality is seen ultimately as consisting only of the interactions of the universe's basic building blocks.

Those who make this claim are perhaps encouraged by the fact that ontological reductionism is indeed valid in some rather simple cases.[1] But even from a purely scientific perspective, it is being increasingly recognized that these simple cases do not imply that this kind of reductionism may be applied successfully to all situations. The kind of genetic determinism that characterized many of an earlier generation of geneticists, for example, has given way in the scientific community to a more nuanced appreciation of the role of epigenetic factors.[2] In a comparable way, the reductionist contention of the earlier forms of sociobiology—that all human behavior is simply the product of human genes—has proved very questionable from a scientific perspective.[3]

---

[1]It is, for example, true that the macroscopic properties of gases—expressed in terms of pressure, volume, and temperature by "laws" put forward by scientists of the early modern period—proved, in the early twentieth century, to be reducible in a very straightforward way to the kinetic properties of the atoms or molecules of which gases are made up. Ontological reductionism is clearly justified in this case.

[2]On epigenetics, see chapter 1, note 7.

[3]Sociobiology investigates social behaviors, such as mating patterns, territorial fights, pack hunting, and the hive society of social insects. It argues that just as selection pressure led to animals evolving useful ways of interacting with the natural environment, it led also to the genetic evolution of advantageous social behavior. In itself this insight undoubtedly contains

Over and above specific scientific problems of this kind, a fact often pointed out by participants in the Western science-theology dialogue is important here. This is that the kind of reductionist ideology on which these approaches are based—the idea that some property of an entity is "nothing but" the properties of its component parts—is philosophically naïve. At the very least, these critics say, we need to acknowledge that reducibility of the theory applicable to one level of complexity to that of another, lower, level of complexity, is far from being an evident truth. If we want to discuss animal behavior, for example, we seem to need concepts like *predator* and *sexuality,* which cannot be related in any way to the properties of the component parts of which animals are made up. These concepts relate to properties of complex wholes, and are only applicable to those wholes.

From observations of this kind, many within the dialogue have been led to speak about a hierarchy of complexity in the universe, with each more complex level manifesting new *emergent* features that cannot be described completely in terms of the properties of lower levels. Not only, they point out, have aspects of living things proved not to be susceptible to being described completely in terms of physics and chemistry, so that life must be seen as a "new emergent" property of the universe, but in addition (they also point out), there are good reasons to believe that aspects of human consciousness should be seen as another "new emergent," representing a higher level of complexity than simple life.

an important element of truth. Nevertheless, in its early forms (as in the earlier work of E. O. Wilson) sociobiology was often excessively reductionist. Criticism from within the scientific community by people like Richard Lewontin and Stephen Jay Gould focused on early sociobiology's contention that genes play an ultimate role in human behavior and that traits such as aggressiveness can be explained by biology rather than a person's social environment. Sociobiologists have in more recent times generally recognized the weight of this criticism and have responded by acknowledging the complex relationship between nature and nurture.

The philosophical concept of emergence has thus allowed life and thought to be seen as just as "real" as are atoms and molecules. The higher levels of complexity that are involved in the former are simply not reducible to the lower levels of complexity of the latter, and causality must be seen in terms of a model that is far more subtle than the one assumed by the reductionists. The "strong" emergentists,[4] in particular, stress that "top down" causality also exists. Not only, according to this view, does the brain affect the mind, but in addition the mind affects the brain, so that complex "feedback loops" need to be acknowledged.

This debate about emergence is, it must be admitted, far from finished, and changes of emphasis and new insights will no doubt enrich it in years to come.[5] What seems likely, however, is that whatever new factors are taken into account in future discussion, two aspects of this analysis will remain broadly unchanged. The first of these—a welcome one for religious believers—is the recognition that ontological reductionism is far from being a self-evident truth. The qualities that we associate with the term *soul*—thought, free will, and so on—are not simply to be dismissed as ultimately unreal. The second factor may not, however, at first seem so welcome, and because of this it requires fuller exploration.

This second factor is the growing consensus among the defenders of emergence that the validity of their arguments does not

---

[4]Some reductionist assumptions are shared by those who espouse what has been called "weak" emergence theory, in which the reality of emergent mental processes is recognized but it is still assumed that physical processes provide a complete causal explanation. This term and the arguments of those who advocate it are described in Philip Clayton, "The Conceptual Foundations of Emergence," in Philip Clayton and Paul Davies, eds., *The Re-Emergence of Emergence: The Emergentist Hypothesis From Science to Religion* (Oxford: Oxford University Press, 2006), 1–31.

[5]The current state of debate is well represented in the essays in Clayton and Davies, *The Re-Emergence of Emergence*.

require the kind of *vitalistic* approach that speaks in terms of some kind of substance (in the philosophical sense) being *added* to the basic building blocks of nature in order to give rise to life and to what it is to be human.[6] The emergence, first of life and then of intelligent self-conscious beings, is, according to the consensus among emergence theorists, a straightforward *naturalistic* outcome of the way the universe was at its very beginning, and arises purely from holistic factors in complex systems.

This has been well put by the physicist, Paul Davies, in terms of his own understanding of these holistic factors. There is, he says,

> no compelling reason why the fundamental laws of nature have to refer only to the lowest level of entities, i.e. the fields and particles that we presume to constitute the elementary stuff from which the universe is built. There is no logical reason why new laws may not come into operation at each emergent level in nature's hierarchy of organization and complexity. . . . It is not necessary to suppose that these higher level organizing principles carry out their marshalling of the system's constituents by deploying mysterious new forces especially for the purpose, which would indeed be tantamount to vitalism. . . . [Instead, they] could be said to harness the existing interparticle forces, rather than supplement

---

[6]This kind of vitalism in fact has its origins in the kind of "substance" metaphysics that is characteristically assumed in Western theology. See the introductory comments in William Bechtel and Robert C. Richardson, "Vitalism," in Edward Craig, ed., *The Routledge Encyclopedia of Philosophy* (London: Routledge, 1998). It should be noted, perhaps, that vitalism in its classic nineteenth-century application to biology did not arise primarily through theological motives but—as in the work of Hans Driesch and Henri Bergson—was essentially philosophical in nature. For a brief account of vitalist views of evolutionary emergence, see Arthur Peacocke, *God and the New Biology* (London: J. M. Dent and Sons, 1986), 73ff.

them, and in so doing alter the behavior in a holistic fashion. Such organizing principles need therefore in no way contradict the underlying laws of physics as they apply to the constituent parts of the system.[7]

Because of this kind of rebuttal of vitalism, the present stress on emergent properties tends to challenge the kind of quasi-vitalist argument sometimes encountered in Christian circles, in which a naturalistic account of the physical development of the cosmos is accepted, but "gaps" are perceived in things like life and human mental capacities. These gaps, it is assumed, must be filled by God from beyond the physical world. But as we have noted in the case of the apparent "soul" gap that such people tend to cite as the main example of something that requires vitalist explanation, a simplistic dualistic notion of the soul—as something essentially independent of, and added to, the body—is not actually compatible with a Christian anthropology rooted in biblical and patristic perspectives. Rather, what we refer to as the soul is, for such an anthropology, a component of our embodied existence. It might be better, some have suggested, to speak not of the "soul," as though it were an entity existing independently of the body, but instead of "embodied soulishness," a term which, it is claimed, can affirm the reality of all that is usually associated with the term *soul* while avoiding any kind of dualism.[8] (As we shall see, however, while there is merit in this suggestion, and there is certainly validity in the reasons for its being made, there are aspects of the functioning of the soul that may need to be understood in a more subtle way than this.)

---

[7]Paul Davies, *The Cosmic Blueprint* (London: Unwin Hyams, 1987), 143.

[8]See Warren Brown and Brad D. Strawn, *The Physical Nature of Christian Life* (Cambridge: Cambridge University Press, 2012), 28–48.

Some have suggested that a model related to electronic computers may now help us to understand the anthropology of traditional Christianity. This model is one in which the distinction between body and soul is thought about in terms of the distinction between hardware and software in a computer. Without the software (the soul), the hardware (the body) has no real purpose. Without the hardware, however, the software has no natural means of functioning. This may not (as we shall see in the next chapter) be a very complete analogy for us. It does, however, point towards something of great importance in traditional Christian understanding that is often ignored or downplayed in certain kinds of thinking that stress the importance of the "immortal soul." This is that our eternal life—our *eschatological* state—will not consist of being a disembodied soul but—as traditional Christian teaching has always affirmed—will involve a "resurrection body" of some kind. Our natural state—both in this world and in the age to come—is, in this perspective, not one in which our "software" alone can constitute our being. Our earthly bodies and our resurrection bodies are both appropriate to our created nature, constituting the proper and normal "hardware" through which our "software" functions can operate.[9]

This eschatological aspect of our thinking about the soul does, however, raise questions about one characteristic of the way in which the concept of emergence has been used in the Western science-theology dialogue. Most of the participants in that dialogue speak, almost instinctively, in a way that accepts uncritically the essentially *materialist* framework of our current scientific culture.

[9]The question of whether our "soul" functions are operative in the period between our deaths and the beginning of the functioning of our resurrection bodies has been answered differently by different Orthodox authors. Yet even those who affirm such "intermediate" functioning usually recognize that it is not the "natural" functioning associated with the union of body and soul, but is only possible because of divine grace.

They focus on how human mental capacities emerge from the matter of the brain but not on how, in a theological perspective, matter has its origin in the mind of God. This means that they have usually rejected any form of philosophical *idealism,* in which mind is given priority over matter.

In certain respects this is rather odd, since this attitude has not always been typical of modern scientists. The early twentieth century astrophysicists, James Jeans and Arthur Eddington, for example, wrote popular books that interpreted science in an idealistic spirit, arguing that modern physics seemed to require such an interpretation. The later avoidance of such interpretation among scientists may perhaps be due to the effect of the philosophical attack on Eddington's and Jeans' views made by Susan Stebbing.[10] This widely-read criticism was such that later scientists—even if their instincts were of an idealist kind—became wary of trespassing on philosophical territory in which they had little or no formal training. That Western theological scholars should have followed them in this wariness is, however, less easily understandable, except perhaps in terms of the common misunderstanding of the views of the most famous idealist of the modern era, the eighteenth-century Anglican bishop, George Berkeley.

This misunderstanding has been pointed out by Keith Ward, who analyzes the way in which people like John Polkinghorne—who see it as necessary to avoid "retreating into Bishop Berkeley's idealist castle[11]—in fact take up a stance that does not sit easily with classical Christian theism. Ward explains that Berkeley did not claim—as many think he did—that "physical objects do not exist, and that everything is in human minds, so that the world disappears when humans are not looking at it." This view may

[10]L. Susan Stebbing, *God and the Physicists* (Harmondsworth: Penguin, 1937).

[11]John Polkinghorne, *One World,* 109.

constitute one form of idealism but, as Ward comments, to assume that Berkeley thought in this way is "a complete misunderstanding." Berkeley, in assuming that physical objects cannot exist without some perceiving mind, was, says Ward, essentially saying that "if there is a physical world independent of humans, it must exist in the mind of God . . . though not exactly as it is perceived by humans." This position is, he observes, certainly idealist in the sense that matter "exists as the content of mental acts, and could not exist on its own." Nevertheless, he goes on, this position "is not very far, if it is any distance at all, from classical Christian theism" since the Christian necessarily believes that "God who is not material, can exist without a material universe, but matter cannot exist without God. If God is anything like a mind—and God is said to know, to act, to have purposes and to be wise—then Christians must believe that mind can exist without matter."[12]

Ward does not, we must note, ignore the evidence that leads people to speak of the emergence of mind from matter in created beings. He points out, however, that what this evidence entails— what Polkinghorne calls "the psychosomatic integrity of human beings"[13]—may preclude certain types of dualism but does not require quite the kind of wholesale anti-dualism that many seem to suppose it does.

Ward points out—as Polkinghorne does also—that the Christian eschatological hope (at least as often expressed) is for the existence of a human mind in a resurrection body that is in some respects discontinuous with the body of our present existence. Where he differs from Polkinghorne, however, is in his use of this hope as an argument for a kind of dualism. The Christian eschatological understanding, he argues, constitutes "one reason

[12]Keith Ward, "Bishop Berkeley's Castle: John Polkinghorne on the Soul," in Fraser Watts and Christopher C. Knight, eds., *God and the Scientist: Exploring the Work of John Polkinghorne* (Farnham: Ashgate, 2012), 127.

[13]John Polkinghorne, *One World*, 91.

why a dualistic view is so important, because it allows my mental properties to be transferred to a different form of embodiment" in the world to come. The only relevant form of close similarity here, he argues "is mental, not bodily. Embodiment may be essential to being fully human, but [in the traditional Christian eschatological understanding] there are different forms of embodiment possible for the same person. It follows that my mental properties and capacities cannot be wholly dependent on the structure of this brain, since this brain will certainly cease to exist and will not simply be replicated in the world to come."[14]

Ward compares the view that arises from this insight to the "dual aspect monism" that philosophers like John Searle have advocated. Ward judges this form of monism to be ambiguous, however, since "it is consistent with the belief that matter is the real causal basis of mind." Even if it is acknowledged that minds are different from brains, he argues, dual-aspect monism is not in itself incompatible with the view that "minds cannot exist without the brains that give rise to them, and minds cannot simply be decoupled and transferred to other forms of embodiment." Instead of permitting this ambiguity, Ward prefers to speak of *dual-aspect idealism*, "which postulates that minds can exist without brains, can be transferred to other forms of embodiment, and indeed that matter exists primarily to enable certain sorts of mental properties to be expressed, so that in the end minds have causal and ontological priority over matter. . . . What matters is that matter has been created to enable minds to emerge and to exist, as natural parts of the cosmic process."[15]

There are, it should be said, aspects of Ward's thinking about this issue that Orthodox Christians will find less than entirely convincing. One of these arises from the way in which Ward seems

[14]Ward, "Bishop Berkeley's Castle," 130.
[15]Ward, "Bishop Berkeley's Castle," 130.

to see the "world to come" in purely temporal terms—as something that happens "after" this life, so that "decoupling" the mind from the earthly body is essential if it is to be "re-embodied" in a different, body. This is, however, to fail to see that "eternal life" may relate, not to what is sometimes called "sempiternity"—time going on for ever—but to eternity in the sense of something that transcends the ordinary temporal process.[16]

Another potential problem with Ward's argument arises from the observation that, when speaking of the kind of mind that can, in theistic perspective, clearly exist without embodiment—God's mind—he seems to think that human minds are directly comparable to it. This is something that we Orthodox Christians—with our apophatic aversion to comparing God to created things—may well question.

A third issue, related to this, is that there is a sense in which Ward's view of mind is more an early modern philosophical one than one rooted in traditional theological anthropology. Orthodox thinking, as we have already noted, has an understanding of mind that makes a distinction between what is commonly thought of as the mind—the memory and the discursive, conceptualizing, logical faculty (*dianoia* in Greek)—and the intellect (*nous*), which provides direct, intuitive knowledge. It is the latter that is seen in patristic thinking as the "eye" of the soul (*psychē*), and there is

---

[16]This is a complex issue, but in the context of our present discussion we must remember two things. The first is that Orthodoxy has a very nuanced view of how time should be understood. This is especially the case in the thinking of St Maximos the Confessor—see, e.g., the analysis in Sotiris Mitalexis, *Ever-Moving Response: A Contemporary Reading of Maximus the Confessor's Theory of Time* (Cambridge: James Clarke and Co., 2018). The second is that, in the fourth gospel, Jesus is reported as implying that eternal life is already present in this life to the extent that it conforms to a simple definition: "that they may know you, the only true God, and Jesus Christ whom you have sent" (John 17.3).

no straightforward equivalence between the soul and the mind of the kind that Ward seems to assume.

Despite these issues, however, Ward's basic argument for a kind of re-appropriation of Berkeleyan thinking remains an interesting one from an Orthodox perspective. Indeed, in certain respects his thinking about the world to come manifests parallels with the sacramentalist aspect of Orthodox thinking that are only rarely found in Western Christian thinking. This can be seen in the way in which he explains why it is that adoption of Berkeley's views "is not at all to denigrate the physical. Berkeley's souls are not disembodied, as Plato's arguably were. They are properly and naturally expressed in a physical environment, in which they come to be and grow." In the eschatological state, he says, souls "will never be wholly disembodied, but the form of their embodiment will be such that matter will be, as it is not yet, the unimpeded instrument and sacrament of spirit."[17] (This sense of how the sacramental character of created things will be fully manifested only in the eschatological state has important ramifications, as we shall see, for the Orthodox understanding of divine action.)

In the light of both the shortcomings and genuine insights of Ward's approach, we must ask whether we can follow him in his basic argument without succumbing to the simplistic aspects of his understanding of the mind and of eternal life. It is to this question that we shall turn in the next chapter, and my suggestion will be that there are good theological reasons for seeing Ward's argument as applying to the *nous* but not to the other mental faculties that we Orthodox see as distinct from it. This has the advantage, I shall argue, of enabling us to see these other faculties in terms of emergent properties that are dependent upon physical brain processes, while at the same time affirming Ward's basic argument for at least some kind of idealism.

[17]Ward, "Bishop Berkeley's Castle," 136.

chapter seven

THE HUMAN MIND IN THIS WORLD AND THE NEXT

What is it to be a human being? For the scientist, it is to be the most complex part of the universe known to us, with mental and creative capacities continuous with—but far more extensive than—those known in other creatures. In this sense, while humanity's central geographical position in the cosmos disappeared with the downfall of the geocentric model of the universe, its centrality in terms of complexity undoubtedly remains.

For the Christian theological scholar, this scientific picture makes perfect sense on one level at least, since most Christian traditions—following the creation accounts in the Book of Genesis—have seen humanity as the culmination of God's act of creation. This understanding has been particularly characteristic of our Orthodox theology, and not only because that theology has, as we have seen, a strong sense of the human capacity to know God directly in an intuitive way through the *nous*, but also because Orthodox theological anthropology is informed by another notion that we need to take into account.

This is the belief—prominent in the work of several modern Orthodox authors—that humans have a very particular role as *mediators* between God and his creation. A few recent scholars have explored this notion in terms of the ancient idea of man as microcosm. More often, however, they have expressed it in terms of the kind of sacramental cosmology emphasized by people like Father Alexander Schmemann. In this approach, what is stressed is that the sacramental life of the Church, culminating in the Eucharist, is a revelation of the true nature of God's creation.

Those who think in this way tend to understand the fall recounted in the Book of Genesis in a very particular way, which has its roots in the thinking of St Maximos the Confessor. They see this Genesis narrative as referring essentially to the way in which human self-centeredness distorts both the relationship between humans and God and the way created things function within that relationship. Thus, for example, Schmemann says that "The world was given to man by God for 'food'—as means of life; yet life was meant to be communion with God; it had not only its end but its full content in him." For this reason, he goes on, "to eat, to be alive, to know God and thus be in communion with him were one and the same thing. The unfathomable tragedy of Adam was that he ate for its own sake. More than that he ate 'apart' in order to be independent of him."[1]

Schmemann's attitude here is comparable to that of another major Orthodox writer of the present time, Metropolitan John (Zizioulas) of Pergamon. Like Schmemann, Zizioulas takes up Maximos' notion of the fall as essentially a shift away from from being God-centered towards being self-centered. Zizioulas speaks of the Christian life as involving a "reversal of Adam's attitude, who took the world as his own and referred it to himself."[2] In this

---

[1] Alexander Schmemann, *Great Lent* (Crestwood, NY: St Vladimir's Seminary Press, 1973), 94–95.

[2] John Zizioulas, "Man the Priest of Creation," in A. Walker and C. Carras, eds., *Living Orthodoxy in the Modern World* (London: SPCK, 1996), 185.

perspective, the path back from the fall involves the development of an attitude of referring everything in the world back to God.

A modern way of speaking about this attitude is that in which humans are described as *priests of creation*. This phrase may seem at first sight to be entirely appropriate to the Orthodox under-standing of the role of humans as mediators, not least because it picks up another patristic theme that was expressed most clearly by St Leontius of Cyprus in the seventh century, using the imagery of Psalm 18 (LXX) and of the Song of the Three Young Men in the deuterocanonical part of the Book of Daniel. The creation, says Leontius, "does not venerate the Maker directly and by itself, but it is through me that the heavens declare the glory of God; through me the moon worships God, through me the stars glorify him, through me the waters and showers of rain, the dew and all creation, venerate God and give him glory."[3]

If at one level, however, the phrase "priest of creation" seems entirely appropriate to this kind of vision, at another level it may be problematical, at least in the usage of some who have advocated it. Elizabeth Theokritoff has noted that this phrase was not actually part of patristic usage, and she cautions that in practice it is used in different ways by different modern writers, who do not always in their usage convey the fullness of what the patristic writers said about mediation. In particular, she is wary of the way in which some modern users of the phrase seem to see the non-human parts of creation as having no value over and above their practical or spiritual use by human beings.

With her own strong sense of the ecological attitudes appro-priate to Orthodoxy, Theokritoff insists that the non-human parts of creation must be seen as having an *intrinsic* value in the sight of God, and she sees this as being expressible in "priest of creation"

---

[3]Leontius of Cyprus, *Fifth Homily of Christian Apologetic against the Jews, and on the Icons* (PG 93:1604B).

language only if this term is used carefully. In this context she points with approval to one particular way of speaking of the role of humanity in offering creation to God: that which has been developed in recent years by Alexei Nesteruk.

Taking up the patristic notion of the Father, Son, and Holy Spirit as the three *hypostases* (persons) of the Holy Trinity, Nesteruk has advocated an expansion of the notion of *hypostasis* of the kind that was developed originally in the work of St Leontius of Byzantium. This expansion speaks in terms of humans bestowing personal existence on inanimate things in such a way that humans can offer the creation to God.[4] This offering is understood by Nesteruk as being brought about in part through the work of the scientist, which he sees as "para-eucharistic"[5] insofar as it involves the universe's being "offered to God by man through his 'cosmic liturgy' of knowledge."[6]

Nesteruk's use of the term *hypostasis* may, Theokritoff observes, seem "initially opaque."[7] Despite this, she sees it as potentially important because of its way of stressing that humans have "a concrete personal existence involving a sense of self and of otherness." We humans are, she says, able to relate to each other, to God, and to the rest of creation, and this capacity "enables us to *relate creation to God*." In Nesteruk's interpretation of Leontius, she goes on, we humans are seen as "bringing the rest of creation into the hypostatic mode of existence that has been bestowed on

[4]For a good brief summary of this understanding see Alexei Nesteruk, "The Universe as Hypostatic Inherence in the Logos of God: Panentheism in the Eastern Orthodox Perspective," in Clayton and Peacocke, *In Whom We Live and Move and Have Our Being*, 169–183.

[5]Nesteruk, "The Universe as Hypostatic Inherence in the Logos of God," 183.

[6]Nesteruk "The Universe as Hypostatic Inherence in the Logos of God," 179.

[7]Theokritoff, *Living in God's Creation: Orthodox Perspectives on Ecology* (Crestwood, NY: St Vladimir's Seminary Press, 2005), 235.

us. In order to do this, we do not need to shape things or even have to have direct contact with them: we 'take them up' through our awareness and understanding of them."[8] When used in this way, she suggests, the language of priesthood of creation enables us to affirm not only that the cosmos has been made for humanity, but also that humanity has been made for the cosmos.

This sense of humans having a very specific role within the created order is arguably related to an aspect of what we explored in the last chapter: the question of philosophical *idealism*. This, as we have seen, is a question that is related to the belief of all Christians that the cosmos has its origin in the mind of God.

Part of the background to this question lies in considerations that we have already examined about the need to assess the philosophical notion of scientific realism. As we have noted, philosophers like Mary Hesse and Rom Harré—focusing not on ontology but on structure and reference—have offered more subtle accounts of scientific realism than have usually been seen in theological discussion. We have also seen that if we accept the commonly proposed link between the modes of realism inherent in scientific and theological languages, this more nuanced notion of realism provides a new perspective on the patristic notion of the unknowability of God, as well as having implications for our understanding of created things. It points us towards what we might call *apophatic critical realism* in our understanding of the character of both scientific and theological language usage.

One of the insights that arise from this apophatic critical realism is that we need to be extremely wary of what (in the scientific context) Harré has called the "metaphysical predilections"[9] that tend to lead us to assume a particular ontology in a way that cannot be justified philosophically. This points to the need to question

[8]Elizabeth Theokritoff, *Living in God's Creation*, 235.
[9]Harré, *Varieties of Realism*, 316.

the way in which many Western participants in the science-theology dialogue take a stance about the ontology of the world that is implicitly *materialist*.[10] They may usually add a theistic gloss to the atheistic version of materialism by positing that the "stuff" of the world has been brought into existence, and is sustained in existence, by God's will. Nevertheless, they are in other respects in complete agreement with atheistic materialists about the nature of physical reality. They posit, at least implicitly, an essentially autonomous set of entities that, once in being, are connected to the divine mind only in the sense that God has chosen to uphold in being their natural properties.

This common assumption has often led, as we have seen, to a sense among Western theological scholars that the human mind—even if seen as real in the sense of being an "emergent property" of the universe—is entirely dependent on the physical brain for its existence. Further, their focus on scientific insights into brain functioning has meant that the notion of the "mind" that is typically used by them is, from an Orthodox perspective, a simplistic one. It focuses on the processes seen in modern scientific discussion as constitutive of that functioning, i.e., those associated with sense perception, memory, reasoning, and emotion. This focus means that unconscious processes are treated in a very limited way. While there has in recent decades been recognition by scientists of some of these processes, this recognition is limited to the reality of what is called the "cognitive unconscious."[11] There has been little or no consideration of other unconscious processes, whether of the kind hypothesized in therapeutic

---

[10]The "stuff" of which the cosmos is presumed to consist is, of course, no longer taken by materialists to be the stuff of the pre-atomic or atomic models of reality, but is seen in terms of quantum mechanical insights.

[11]This term first came into widespread use through the influence of an article by John F. Kihlstrom: "The Cognitive Unconscious," *Science* 237 (1987): 1445–52.

practice[12] or of the kind on which this chapter will concentrate: that which in patristic theology was expressed in terms of the concept of the *nous*.

Here, the views of St Gregory of Nyssa point to the way in which much that seems to be taken for granted in discussion of the mind within the modern Western science-theology dialogue is challenged, in a fascinating way, if we assume the reality of something like the *nous* as it was conceived by him and by many of his contemporaries. In what follows I shall argue, in particular, that acceptance of the reality of this faculty will, in two related ways, significantly affect the way in which the notion of *mind* is used theologically. The first of these relates to the issue of the emergence of the mental from the physical; the second relates to our understanding of the human condition in the "world to come."

The term *nous*, as we have noted, is usually translated into English as *intellect*. But it refers to something different in character from what is usually now understood by that word. The *nous* was seen, in ancient and medieval times, not as the seat of discursive reasoning, but as the direct intuitive faculty that is necessary for understanding what is true or real. There are, in fact, many distinct, if related, understandings to be found in different authors.[13] In a religious context—both Christian and

---

[12]As one commentator has noted, notions of the unconscious that have arisen through the practice of psychoanalysis or of analytical psychology have usually been rejected in academic or scientific circles as "largely unfalsifiable" (James S. Uleman, "Introduction," in Ran R. Hassin, James S. Uleman, and John A. Barr, eds., *The New Unconscious* [Oxford: Oxford University Press, 2005], 5). See the comments on this in Christopher C. Knight, "The Psychology of Religion and the Concept of Revelation," *Theology and Science* 14 (2016): 482–494.

[13]The variety to be found was due in part to differences in the use of the term *nous* in the works of Aristotle and Plato. Depending on the Aristotelian or neoplatonic assumptions of late antique and medieval writers, different

Islamic[14]—these include seeing the *nous* as the organ of contemplation, the source of true wisdom. Indeed, in many strands of theological thinking, the *nous* was seen as central to the relationship between the human person and God: the point at which the human mind was in some sense in direct contact with the divine mind. Particularly in Christian theology, however, it was seen as having been diminished in its abilities by the fall, so that the spiritual journey in this life was understood as one of increasingly returning the *nous* to its pre-lapsarian capabilities.

Some Western scholars have wondered why participants in the science-theology dialogue should take the notion of *nous* seriously when it is only rarely considered in modern Western theology and has no place at all in current scientific discourse. The answer lies, I have suggested,[15] at least in part in the difficulty we have in refuting the kind of reductionist analysis in which religious faith is regarded as an illusion rooted in human psychology. If a coherent understanding of religious faith is to be developed in a non-reductionist way, something is needed that provides a link between faith and other aspects of human psychology. The concept of *nous* constitutes, as we shall see, a helpful starting point for thinking about such a link, and the understanding of St Gregory of Nyssa is particularly valuable in this respect.

At one level, Gregory's framework manifests very clear parallels with that to be found in the neoplatonic thinking of Plotinus about the role of the *nous* in spiritual development. As Martin

understandings and emphases are to be found, though these do not significantly alter the conclusions of the present chapter.

[14]Among many others in the medieval Islamic world, the concept of *nous* was important for Al Farabi, Avicenna, and Ibn Rushd (better known in the Western world as Averroes).

[15]Christopher C. Knight, "The Human Mind in This World and the Next: Scientific and Early Theological Perspectives," *Theology and Science* 16 (2018): 151–165.

Laird has observed, both Gregory and Plotinus employ the Platonic motif of the mind's ascent to the Incomprehensible, placing a distinct faculty of union at the apex of this ascent. This summit is seen as being reached only through a process in which the discursive reasoning ability eventually gives way to the direct contemplation that is the function of the *nous*. (As Plotinus puts it, "we put aside all learning," or as Gregory puts it, "every form of comprehension" is abandoned.[16]) Yet a major difference between Plotinus and Gregory is that this ascent is seen by Gregory, not only in terms of Plotinus's neoplatonic understanding of the *nous*, but also in terms of the central Christian concept of *faith*.

Gregory uses the term "faith" (*pistis*), not as it had been used in much early Greek philosophy, in which it had denoted the lowest form of knowledge. Instead, as Laird puts it, he ascribes to faith "qualities which Neoplatonism would reserve for the crest of the wave of *nous*."[17] He goes beyond neoplatonic understanding to stress *relationship* with God, focusing on biblical texts and emphasizing the "sacramental origin and development of faith as well as the transforming character of divine union."[18] There was, in his understanding, both a focus on explicitly Christian concepts and a very clear link between the experience of religious faith and those aspects of the ordinary functioning of the mind that were seen by his non-Christian contemporaries as having their origin in the capacities of the *nous*.

Some may, of course, judge that the philosophical frameworks of the present day require another way of expressing these capacities. Nevertheless Gregory's use of the notion of the *nous* suggests that some comparable concept is still needed if we are to provide a philosophical basis for combatting reductionism in relation to

[16]Martin Laird, *Gregory of Nyssa and the Grasp of Faith: Union, Knowledge, and Divine Presence* (Oxford: Oxford University Press, 2004), 127.

[17]Laird, *Gregory of Nyssa*, 2.

[18]Ibid., 128.

the link between mental functioning and religious faith. Even if only for this reason, therefore, the concept seems worthy of consideration.

Combatting reductionism has, as we have noted, been a major pre-occupation of the Western science-theology dialogue of recent decades, and the notion of *emergence* has been a central one in undertaking this task.[19] This notion has been applied, however, less to refute the reductionist attempt to reduce religious faith to psychology than to the attempt to reduce psychology itself to chemical and electrical processes in the brain.

In this latter context, the reality of mental experience has frequently been defended by insisting that the only causality acknowledged in reductionist analysis—the "bottom up" kind in which it is assumed that that the mind is "caused" by the brain—must be seen as being supplemented by "top down" causal effects, so that the mind also affects the brain, and the relationship between the two is seen in terms of complex feedback loops. According to this "strong emergentist" view, the qualities often associated with the term *soul*—discursive thought, the sense of free will, and so on— are not simply to be dismissed as epiphenomena with no ultimate reality. What is usually dismissed, however, even by those who stress emergence in this way, is the notion that these qualities can have any reality apart from the body. The result has been that the dualistic notion of the *soul* as a distinct entity has often, in recent thinking, been replaced by an understanding that is summed up in Warren Brown's term, *embodied soulishness*.[20]

As we have already noted, there are some, in this context, who have suggested that it is helpful to think about the distinc-

---

[19]The current state of debate about emergence is well represented in the essays in Clayton and Davies, *The Re-Emergence of Emergence*.

[20]For some of Brown's more recent thinking about this concept, see Brown and Strawn, *The Physical Nature of Christian Life*.

tion between the body and the mind in terms of the distinction between body and software in an electronic computer. This analogy—despite shortcomings that we shall note presently—has been helpful in making Western theological scholars wary of the notion of the eschatological existence of disembodied souls, which is now often seen as untenable because it assumes software functioning without appropriate hardware. It has thus provided these scholars with a plausible argument for upholding the traditional theological concept of the eschatological state, in which humans in the "age to come" are seen, not as disembodied souls, but as possessing *resurrection bodies*.

Our natural state—both in this world and the next—is not, they have argued, one in which our "software" alone can constitute our being. Our earthly bodies and our resurrection bodies are both appropriate to our created nature, constituting, in different environments, the "hardware" through which our "software" functions can operate. Moreover, since different types of computer hardware can be used to operate any particular software, this analogy has allowed these scholars to conceive of the resurrection body as significantly different from the earthly one. (While this notion is sometimes seen in the West as a novel one,[21] it was, as we shall see, a belief that was common in Eastern patristic thought.)

Within the Western science-theology dialogue, it has perhaps been John Polkinghorne who has focused most clearly on the way in which the traditional understanding of the resurrection of the body is now reinforced by scientific analogies of this kind.[22]

---

[21]This sense of novelty exists because, as we shall note presently, Western Christian perspectives on the resurrection body—based on the views of early Western authors like Tertullian—are wrongly assumed to have been accepted throughout the Christian world.

[22]See, e.g., John Polkinghorne, *The God of Hope and the End of the World* (London: SPCK, 2002).

This eschatological aspect of theological thinking, however, raises important questions about the way in which the concept of emergence has been used by him and by many others. For it is observable that most participants in the Western dialogue speak, almost instinctively, in a way that accepts uncritically an aspect of the materialist framework of our current scientific culture. They focus, as we have noted, on how the human mind emerges from the matter of the brain but very little on how, in a theological perspective, matter has its origin in the "mind of God." This means that they have rejected any form of philosophical *idealism,* in which mind is given ontological priority over matter.

In certain respects, as we have already observed, the prevalence of this anti-idealistic view within the dialogue is curious, since it is not an attitude that is entailed by science and it has not always been typical of modern scientists. Moreover, as Keith Ward has argued, the Christian eschatological understanding may be seen as constituting a reason for retaining at least some kind of dualistic view, because it allows mental properties to be transferred to a different form of embodiment in the world to come.

In assessing Ward's views here, it is important in an Orthodox context to recognize that, in trying to rehabilitate a kind of neo-Berkeleyan form of idealism, he is attempting to develop an understanding comparable to that held by at least some patristic writers. A figure particularly relevant in this respect is St Gregory of Nyssa, whose thinking about the *nous*—as Joshua Schooping has shown[23]—exhibits interesting parallels, not only with Berkeleyan idealism, but also with the quasi-idealist metaphysics of the quantum physicist, David Bohm.

---

[23]Joshua Schooping, "Touching the Mind of God: Patristic Christian Thought on the Nature of Matter," *Zygon: Journal of Religion and Science* 50 (2015): 583–603.

Gregory was not, of course, attempting to answer the same questions (arising from quantum mechanics) as those addressed by Bohm. He was concerned with a question much asked in his own time: that of how an immaterial principle, God, could create the material universe. Gregory's answer to this question was, as George Karamanolis puts it, "that the question itself is misguided, because the world is not material at all." Rather, for Gregory, the world "is constituted of reasons or qualities . . . which are generated in the divine mind and are recognized in the human mind. This does not mean that Gregory denies the existence of material entities. All he denies is the independent existence to matter."[24]

Gregory's understanding is based on the notion that what ultimately exists is a set of mental realities that relate to the qualities we perceive in created things. For Gregory these exist—and always have existed—in God's mind. God, he says, "established for the creation of beings all things through which matter is constituted: light, heavy, dense, rare, soft, resistant, humid, dry, cold, hot, color, shape, outline, extension. All these are in themselves concepts [*ennoiai*] and bare thoughts [*psila noēmata*].None of them is matter on its own, but they become matter when they combine with each other."[25]

As Karamanolis notes, this focus on qualities is "not an *ad hoc* answer to the question of the nature of matter but rather part of a fairly sophisticated theory that permeates Gregory's entire work."[26] In some of his works, Gregory calls these qualities *logoi* (a term which, as we shall note presently, was later developed by St Maximos the Confessor to express an explicitly christological understanding of the cosmos). For Gregory, "none of the things

---

[24]George Karamanolis, *The Philosophy of Early Christianity* (Durham: Acumen, 2013), 106.

[25]Gregory of Nyssa, *Apology for Hexameron* (PG 44:69C), in the translation given in Karamanolis, *The Philosophy of Early Christianity*, 102.

[26]Karamanolis, *The Philosophy of Early Christianity*, 102.

that pertains to the body on its own [is] a body, not shape, not color, not weight, not extension, not size, nor any of the other things regarded as qualities, but each of them is a logos and their combination and unity with each other makes a body ... these qualities which complement the body are grasped by the intellect and not by sense perception."[27]

In this passage, Karamanolis observes, it is Gregory's understanding of the *nous* (intellect) that is central. Gregory, he says, "makes clear that bodies are intelligible to the extent that they are made up of intelligible entities, the qualities or *logoi*, which are hosted by the divine intellect but also by the human intellect. While creation of sensible, corporeal entities amounts to the combination of the *logoi* of God, we, humans, in turn get to know these entities by combining the logoi that make them up."[28]

Two aspects of Gregory's thinking here are likely to seem problematic for scientifically-literate scholars of the present day. One is his stress on "qualities" of a kind that we now think of as the outcome of factors explicable by "laws of nature" rather than as things in themselves or mental ideas. (Colors, for example, we see in terms of particular distributions of intensity of electromagnetic radiation at various wavelengths.) Even so, this problem is not entirely destructive of Gregory's picture since, if we put aside (as we must) his *specific* examples of what he calls qualities or *logoi*, it is still possible to interpret these *logoi* as incorporating what we now call the laws of nature and the inner essences of created things.

This will especially be the case if we take into account the later expansion of the notion of *logoi* to be found in the work of St Maximos the Confessor, which we shall examine in more detail presently. This understanding is, as we shall see, clearly related to our current understanding of inner essences and the

[27]Quoted by Karamanolis, *The Philosophy of Early Christianity*, 104.
[28]Karamanolis, *The Philosophy of Early Christianity*, 104.

laws of nature, since—as Metropolitan Kallistos of Diokleia has put it—it is based on the notion that "Christ the creator Logos has implanted in every thing a characteristic logos, a 'thought' or 'word' which is God's intention for that thing, its inner essence which makes it distinctively itself[.]"[29]

The second aspect of Gregory's understanding that may seem problematic to us is his focus on the human mind as what makes perception possible. At first sight, this focus seems to ignore the sense perception that is so important to the usual understanding of scientific objectivity. But we need to recognize that Gregory's anthropology is one in which what he calls the soul proper (*kyrios psychē*) or true soul (*alēthēs psychē*) is intellectual in nature but mixes with our material nature *through* the senses. For Gregory, it is not the senses that perceive, but rather the *nous* that perceives through the senses.

Even from a purely scientific perspective, we should not dismiss this notion, since we can see clear reflections of it in the modern psychology of perception, which stresses the way in which our perceptions rely not just on our sensory capacities but also on the mind's way of interpreting the data that come through those capacities.[30] In Gregory's understanding, however, we find something more distinctly philosophical and theological than this. He believes, as Karamanolis puts it, that "the intellect, *nous*, pervades all sense organs and permeates the entire body and renders the entire human nature rational, and in this sense, similar to God."[31]

[29]Kallistos Ware, Bishop of Diokleia, "God Immanent yet Transcendent: The Divine Energies according to Saint Gregory Palamas," in Clayton and Peacocke, *In Whom We Live and Move and Have our Being*, 160.

[30]For a general review of the scientific background to the psychology of perception, see Simon Grondin, *Psychology of Perception* (Basel: Springer, 2016).

[31]Karamanolis, *The Philosophy of Early Christianity*, 212, referring to Gregory of Nyssa, *On the Making of Man* 6.1 (PG 44:140A).

This understanding is—as Karamanolis notes—rooted in the secular philosophy of Gregory's time, displaying "striking affinities with the views of Plotinus and Porphyry."[32]

This ancient philosophical framework does not, of course, have much appeal to some present day Christians. But as we have noted in our discussion of natural theology, we need to recognize that the theological thinking of all creative theologians, in all periods, is inevitably expressed in terms of the philosophy of the writer's own time. It is often only from the perspective of a later period that we can begin to make a distinction between what is central to what is being expressed—the "theological instinct" so to speak—and the philosophical framework and (sometimes flawed) reasoning through which that instinct has been expressed. Applying this to Gregory's arguments, we can see that the philosophical framework that he adopted and adapted, while creating difficulties for some in our own time, may still be instructive in terms of the idealist theological instinct that he seems to want to express. This will be particularly the case when we take into account three aspects of Gregory's thinking that evoke aspects of modern scientific understanding.

One of these—which we have noted in the context of Karamanolis' and Schooping's observations—is that there are clear resemblances between Gregory's understanding of reality and the much later understanding of George Berkeley,[33] which has been defended by Keith Ward and others as consonant with modern

---

[32]Karamanolis, *The Philosophy of Early Christianity*, 105.

[33]Karamanolis himself actually sees more resemblances in certain respects to the perspectives of John Locke. But other historians of philosophy have seen Gregory much more in terms of his anticipation of the Berkeleyan understanding. See, e.g., the different views expressed in Darren Hibbs, "Was Gregory of Nyssa a Berkeleyan Idealist?" *British Journal of Philosophy* 13 (2005): 425–35; Jonathan Hill, "Gregory of Nyssa, Material Substance and Berkeleyan Idealism," *British Journal of Philosophy* 17 (2009): 653–83.

scientific perspectives. The second is that even if aspects of the human mind should be seen as emergent properties of matter, the mind as a whole has certain characteristics that do not straightforwardly fit into the usual emergentist and evolutionary frameworks. Our abstract mathematical ability, for example, has often been seen as something that is difficult to fit into the framework provided by evolutionary psychology in its usual "blind watchmaker" form, since this ability seems to go far beyond what was able to contribute to the survival of our ancestors.[34] This has been seen by some as indicating an intrinsic affinity between the human mind and the mind of God.[35]

The third reason for examining the human mind more closely in relation to questions about idealism is, however, possibly the most important, at least in the context of the science-theology dialogue. It is that scientific perspectives suggest that, even if no acceptable form of idealism has yet been developed, something akin to what Ward has called "dual-aspect idealism" may still be required.

The point here is that the role of the observer in "creating" physical reality is a major issue in the interpretation of quantum mechanics. While astonishingly fruitful in making predictions at

[34]This observation does not imply that an evolutionary framework must be abandoned, but it does suggest either some kind of "guiding" of the evolutionary process or else some kind of framework in which the predictability of that framework is seen as part of God's initial design of the whole cosmos. The latter view is advocated in terms of evolutionary convergence in a later chapter of this book, which is based in part on Christopher C. Knight, *The God of Nature*.

[35]In Peter Berger, *A Rumour of Angels: Modern Society and the Rediscovery of the Supernatural* (Harmondsworth: Penguin, 1969), mathematics is viewed as one of the "signals of transcendence" that led Berger to take theological thinking seriously. In a comparable way, the mathematician Roger Penrose, while avoiding any specific theological speculation, has seen mathematics as pointing to some kind of Platonic realm of reality; see Roger Penrose, *The Emperor's New Mind* (Harmondsworth: Penguin, 2001).

the sub-atomic level, this branch of physics has proved extremely difficult to interpret philosophically. It seems to suggest that the world, until observed, consists not of matter in a particular physical state but rather of multiple potentialities described by a wave function. Only one of these potentialities is actuated through the action of an observer, who is said to "collapse the wave function." This understanding leads, however, to counter-intuitive situations, of the kind indicated in the famous paradox articulated by Erwin Schrödinger, who famously asked the question of how we are to understand the situation of a cat, put into a box that has been set up in such a way that there is a fifty per cent probability that the cat will die before the box is opened and the situation observed. As he pointed out, quantum mechanics suggests, counter-intuitively, that the cat is in fact in two states just before the box's opening: one in which it is dead and one in which it is alive. Only when the observation is made is one of these two potentialities actualized.[36]

In the judgment of some, this philosophical problem of the role of the observer in quantum mechanics has only been dealt with in a coherent way through the notion of the "implicate order" that David Bohm has offered,[37] which in certain respects may be seen as a manifestation of the "dual aspect idealism" for which Ward pleads. The widespread rejection of Bohm's understanding by his fellow physicists is not due to its being incompatible with quantum mechanics, on which Bohm was an acknowledged expert. It has been rejected largely, it would seem, because of its metaphysical overtones. Although there has recently been a new wave of interest in Bohm's ideas among physicists, it is still the

[36]For an accessible description of this paradox and a more general introduction to quantum mechanics, see John C. Polkinghorne, *The Quantum World* (Princeton: Princeton University Press, 1985).

[37]David Bohm, *Wholeness and the Implicate Order* (London: Routledge & Kegan Paul, 1980).

case that most of them prefer paradox (or an unfalsifiable "many worlds" interpretation) to the notion that mind and matter should be reinterpreted in a way that is not essentially materialist.

As these factors suggest, Ward's attempt to defend a kind of neo-Berkeleyan scheme manifests interesting parallels with aspects of current scientific thinking as well as echoing an aspect of patristic thinking. Still, in attempting to defend a view comparable to that to be found in this thinking, Ward is not, as we have noted, in complete accord with it. Not only does he apply the concept of "mind" to both humans and God in a way that ignores Orthodoxy's apophatic reluctance to apply to God something understood only in relation to created things, but he also—and more importantly—ignores the way in which the human mind is, in Orthodoxy, understood in a more complex way[38] than is to be found in his own understanding, which seems to be essentially that used by philosophers of the early modern period.[39] This means that his use of the terms *mind* and *soul* as effectively synonymous is, from an Orthodox perspective, simplistic.[40]

These considerations suggest that although Ward may validly be pointing us towards the need for an alternative to the materialist

[38]See especially the chapter "The Psyche and the Nous," in Zoran Vujisic, *The Art and Science of Healing the Soul: A Guide to Orthodox Psychotherapy* (Saarbrucken: VDM Verlag Dr. Muller, 2010), 32–40.

[39]As is often the case with philosophical defenders of idealism, Ward seems to work primarily with a somewhat abstract and pre-scientific notion of what the term *mind* might mean, with no basis in any kind of psychological data. The kind of patristic view that I have outlined, while certainly pre-scientific in the formal sense, was, by contrast, based at least partly on experiential data arising from spiritual experience and from observation of spiritual disciples by their mentors. The result was arguably a rather sophisticated set of psychological insights. See Vujisic, *The Art and Science of Healing the Soul.*

[40]An accessible list of terms used in the eastern patristic tradition—and still used in modern Eastern Orthodoxy—is given (together with further references) in Vujisic, *The Art and Science of Healing the Soul,* 7–14.

framework that he rejects, his own version of that alternative may well be flawed. Admittedly, it remains to be seen whether a better approach could arise through some alternative approach, such as attempting to combine Bohmian metaphysics with a revived or revised interpretation of the *logoi* of created things. Whatever view we take of this possibility, however, one thing seems clear. This is that Ward is correct in believing that any framework for thinking about the concept of *mind* can hardly be adequate, from a theological perspective, if the origin of the universe in the mind of God is effectively ignored in the way that it usually is in the Western science-theology dialogue.

This means that, even if no adequate idealist framework yet exists, we cannot simply dismiss idealist understandings of the created order in the way that is commonly done. Rather, we need to develop a framework within which the intrinsic link between most human mental functioning and the physical body is retained, but at the same time the link between the human mind and the "mind of God" is affirmed far more clearly than when "embodied soulishness" is understood purely in terms of emergence of the mental from the physical.

A coherent development of this sort presents itself, in my judgment, if we treat the *nous* as being in certain respects quite different from other mental capacities. The reason for doing this does not lie only in the patristic understanding of the link between the *nous* and the mind of God, or in the way in which, as we have noted, certain mental capacities—such as our abstract mathematical ability—are difficult to fit into the framework provided by evolutionary psychology in its usual "blind watchmaker" form. It lies also in another aspect of Ward's approach that needs questioning from both a scientific and a theological point of view. This is his assumption—with which Polkinghorne seems to agree—that while the earthly body may be very significantly modified when it is transformed into a resurrection body, the earthly mind will continue much as it is in this life, differing only insofar as certain faculties—such as memory—may be made perfect rather than being (as at present) incomplete and fallible.

The scientific issue here is that most cognitive scientists no longer accept in any straightforward way the analogy in which mental processes constitute the functioning of "software" that will give the same results whatever the hardware is that enables it to function. Important aspects of what we call the mind are, they increasingly stress, not only emergent from, but also *conditioned by,* the physical substrate with which they are associated. This seems to be true, not only in relation to the very specific way in which the brain works, but also—if certain formulations of the notion of *embodied cognition* are accepted[41]—in relation to the interactions between the mind and the rest of the body and between the mind and the world beyond the body. If we accept these insights, then—unless the resurrection body and resurrection cosmos are assumed to be identical to those we experience in

[41]Embodied Cognition is a growing research program in cognitive science that emphasizes the formative role the environment plays in the development of cognitive processes, based on a general theory that cognitive processes develop when a tightly coupled system emerges from real-time, goal-directed interactions between organisms and their environment. The nature of these interactions, it is believed, influences the formation and further specifies the nature of the developing cognitive capacities. Since embodied accounts of cognition have been formulated in a variety of different ways in each of the sub-fields comprising cognitive science, a rich interdisciplinary research program is emerging. The different conceptions arising from different sub-fields are all based, however, on the belief that one necessary condition for cognition is embodiment, where the basic notion of embodiment is broadly understood as the unique way an organism's sensorimotor capacities enable it to successfully interact with its environmental niche. All share a quest for cognitive explanations that capture the manner in which mind, body, and world mutually interact and influence one another to promote an organism's adaptive success.

this life—the "resurrection mind" that will be associated with the new body and its environment will inevitably be rather different from our earthly mind.

The related theological issue here is that, once again, the Christian thinking of the patristic era did not always take the view that seems to be taken for granted in much recent Western discussion, and which is often quasi-instinctive among modern Orthodox. Continuity of our mental faculties in their transition from this world to the next was not, in the patristic era, simply assumed. As we shall see presently when we come to consider divine action, the Eastern patristic tradition often made a firm distinction between our present, biological state—viewed as the result of "the fall"—and the embodied state for which we were originally made and are ultimately destined. In this kind of view, the "original" and eschatological human state is something that has, in some sense, been "covered up" by our present biological state—a view often expressed in the patristic period in terms of an allegorical interpretation of the way in which God is reported to have given "garments of skin" to those expelled from Eden (Gen 3.21).

A useful exploration of this aspect of patristic thinking is that of Panayiotis Nellas. He makes the interesting point that the patristic interpretation of our "garments of skin" relates not only to the physical body—as some scholars have supposed—but also to the soul. What such scholars overlook, he notes, is that writers like St Gregory of Nyssa use the term *garments of skin* to refer to "the entire postlapsarian psychosomatic clothing of the human person."[42] For Gregory, he stresses, the fall has brought about a situation in which the "functions of the soul . . . have also become 'corporeal' along with the body. . . . They form together

---

[42]Panayiotis Nellas, *Deification in Christ: The Nature of the Human Person* (Crestwood, NY: St Vladimir's Seminary Press, 1997), 50 n. 92.

with the body 'the veil of the heart . . . the fleshy covering of the old man.' "[43] A corollary of this perspective would seem to be that when the "garments of skin" are thrown off in our eternal life, *both body and mind are to be transformed.*[44]

Why, we may wonder, do many Christians—including Orthodox ones—tend to be uncomfortable with this idea, and to think in terms of simple continuity of the mind in its transition to the eschatological state? The answer perhaps lies in the widespread hope that eternal life will mean the survival of our "personalities." We need to recognize, however, that in the Orthodox perspective, our usual focus on personality is no more than a kind of egoism, a spiritual blindness and self-centeredness to be overcome. This may be understood in part by making a distinction often made in Orthodox writing: that between being *individuals* and being what we are called to become: *persons in relationship*. As Vladimir Lossky puts it, the one "who is governed by his nature and acts in the strength of his natural qualities, of his character, is the least personal. He sets himself up as an individual, proprietor of his

[43]Nellas, *Deification in Christ*, 50–51. Nellas goes on to examine this perspective as it was developed later in the work of Maximos the Confessor, for whom human rebellion against God "reversed the way in which [the human] psychosomatic organism functioned" (57).

[44]For many in our present era, the particular way in which this discontinuity between our present and eschatological states was perceived may seem unpersuasive. As we have already noted, however, the theological "instinct" that lies behind early understandings may still be worthy of attention even when the particular way in which that instinct was expressed no longer seems to have any persuasive power. In this case, the need for attentiveness to that instinct arises from the scientific insight that human minds are not only inextricably linked to human bodies but also strongly conditioned by them. Given this strong conditioning, it seems to follow that a resurrection body that is significantly different from the earthly one—as assumed by both Ward and Polkinghorne—implies precisely what Gregory of Nyssa seems to have envisaged: an associated mind that is also significantly different from that which we now possess.

own nature, which he pits against the nature of others and regards as his 'me.' "[45] This kind of focus on personhood, coupled with our understanding of the *nous*, would seem to imply that what we nowadays tend to think of as constitutive of our minds and personalities—things like our discursive rational faculty and our memories—may in fact be no more than servants, in this fallen world, of the functioning of the *nous*.

The point here is that our spiritual journey in this world was often seen, in the patristic writings, as having as one of its prime aims the purification of that *nous*: the overcoming of the distortion or darkening of its functions in our present "fallen" state. Often, in Christian literature, the *nous* was described as the "eye" of the soul (*psychē*), and it was the full opening of this eye that was seen as making possible what is sometimes called, in Western Christian theology, the beatific vision.[46] In the light of this understanding, it seems possible to understand the functioning of our "resurrection minds" largely, or even completely, in terms of the resumption of the full functioning of the *nous*. This suggests that the transition to eternal life may in fact involve shedding all mental properties other than the direct intuitive knowledge that arises from the perfected *nous*. (Something of this kind—albeit expressed in different terms—certainly seems to be hinted at in some of the most well known New Testament passages that refer to our eschatological state.[47])

[45]Lossky, *Mystical Theology*, 121f.

[46]There are, we should note, significant differences between the way this vision is interpreted in Western and Eastern Christian traditions. See Fr Theophanes (Constantine), *The Orthodox Doctrine of the Person*, 2nd edn, (Edmonton, Alberta: Timios Prodromis, 2014), ch. 4.

[47]In the Johannine literature, for example, there is a strong sense that eternal life is something that the believer can experience, not only in the future, but also now, in our knowledge of God. Indeed, in the fourth gospel there is the report that Jesus himself not only described but also *defined* eternal life as the state in which we "know . . . the only true God and Jesus

Might it be, therefore, that those of us who are believers in the "world to come" should recognize that, in that world, we may not know *about* anything, or even "think," in the sense in which we usually use that term? Might it be, instead, that we shall simply *know*—directly and intuitively—in the way that mystics, in their most sublime moments in this life, are sometimes said to *know*? If this is valid, then continuity in our existence as unique *persons* will not necessarily involve continuity of much with which we tend to identify ourselves. This continuity—while truly a continuity of our personhood[48]—will involve a transformation of our

Christ" (Jn 14.3). In the Pauline strand of New Testament teaching, the emphasis is, admittedly, different, with a stronger sense of eternal life as belonging to the future. There is also, however, a sense that we are unable in this life to anticipate what our eschatological state will be, and that our knowledge in that state will not simply be an extension of the type of knowledge we have now, but in some sense it will be knowledge in a mode akin to that of God's knowledge. What "God has prepared for those who love him," says Paul, is something that "no eye has seen, nor ear heard, nor the human heart conceived" (1 Cor 2.9). In this life "we see in a mirror dimly," but in eternal life "we will see face to face," knowing "fully," even as we "have been fully known" (1 Cor 13.12).

[48]Some may think that this focus on the role of the *nous* in our eternal life implies that in the world to come we shall in some way become depersonalized. But even if there may be some frameworks of thought in which this kind of focus would make this the case, when this focus is expressed in terms of the theological anthropology that is characteristic of Orthodoxy, there can be no sense of losing our personhood. Olivier Clément, for example, has stressed that, in Orthodox anthropology, salvation is not understood—as it is in some eastern religions—as "dissolution into the vastness of the universe, reabsorption into an impersonal divinity." On the contrary, he says (in a way that is, as we have seen, echoed by Alexei Nesteruk) "humanity must 'personalize' the universe; not save itself by means of the universe, but save it by communicating grace to it" (Olivier Clément, *On Human Being: A Spiritual Anthropology* [London: New City, 2000], 35f.). In its essential nature, says Clément a little later in the same work, "the Church is neither a 'superperson' nor the mere aggregation of inspired individuals. It tends at the same time towards unity and diversity." We must not, he goes on, "think of a person as

whole being that will be far more radical than we often appreciate: a casting aside of our "garments of skin" in both their physical and mental dimensions.

In the perspective provided by this focus on the noetic aspect of our eschatological state, an important insight arises in relation to our use of the concept of the *emergence*, in this life, of our mental faculties from the matter of the brain. This is that there would seem to be no theological problem in seeing most aspects of our present mental functioning—those not intrinsically associated with the *nous*—as emergent properties of our biological bodies, which will cease to function when we die and will not resume their functioning when we receive our resurrection bodies. This permanent cessation of functioning may be seen simply as an aspect of the way in which the casting off of our "garments of skin" at the material level involves also a casting off of all those "functions of the soul" which, for St Gregory of Nyssa and for others among the Fathers, have "become 'corporeal' along with the body."[49]

As we have already noted, in Gregory's understanding there is a spiritual journey, even within this life, in which the greatest saints reach a stage at which "every form of comprehension" has been abandoned in their ascent to God. In terms of the arguments set out in this chapter, it would seem that for all of us, in a comparable way, that abandonment will be a characteristic of the eschatological state to which we are called. In our eternal life we will, through the *nous*, simply *know,* directly and intuitively, in such a way that other kinds of mental functioning—at least in the forms in which we now experience them—will have become redundant.

a cell in a body. Each one is sufficiently important to the risen Christ to be received by him face to face in his kingdom" (p. 49).

[49]Nellas, *Deification in Christ*, 50–51.

chapter eight

THE ORTHODOX DOCTRINE OF CREATION

s we have noted in our exploration of philosophical idealism, St Gregory of Nyssa's thinking included an anticipation of something that was later to be more fully explored by St Maximos the Confessor: the concept of direct human apprehension of the inner essence or principle—*logos*—of each created thing. In this chapter we shall see how this term *logos* (plural *logoi*) is an extremely important one for other aspects of our Orthodox understanding of creation.

Maximos' great contribution here was to stress the way in which the *logos* of each created thing may be seen as directly related to the second person of the Trinity: the *Logos* [Word] spoken of in the Fourth Gospel's prologue (John 1.1–14). In that prologue—on which the doctrine of the incarnation was largely based—the divine *Logos* was explained as what was in existence prior to the act of creation and that in the fullness of time "became flesh" in Jesus Christ. For Maximos, this *Logos* and the *logoi* of created things are so intimately connected that at one point he went as far as to say that "the one Logos is the many logoi, and the many logoi are the one Logos."[1] This linkage means, according

[1]Maximos the Confessor, *Ambiguum* 7, as translated in St Maximus the Confessor, *On the Cosmic Mystery of Jesus Christ*, Popular Patristics Series 25, tr. Paul Blowers and Robert Louis Wilson (Crestwood, NY: St Vladimir's Seminary Press, 2003), 54.

to Fr Andrew Louth, that everything in the universe "has its own meaning in its own *logos*, or principle, but . . . all these *logoi* form a coherent whole, because they all participate in the one *Logos* of God."[2]

Here, Maximos brings into play all the nuances of the Greek term *logos*, and especially those aspects of its meaning which caused it later to be the root of the English term *logical*. As Louth has expressed it, to say that the universe is created by the *Logos* entails, for the speaker of Greek, "that the universe has a meaning, both as a whole and in each of its parts. That 'meaning' is *logos*; everything that exists has its own *logos*, and that *logos* is derived from God the *Logos*. To have meaning, *logos*, is to participate in the *Logos* of God." Behind this, he observes, "lurks the Platonic idea that everything that exists does so "by participating in its form, or idea, which is characterized by its definition; the Greek for definition (in this sense) is, again, *logos*." As he goes on to note, however, by the time these notions reached their most complex and complete Christian expression in the work of Maximos, the Platonic character of this kind of language had already for centuries been adapted to the requirements of the Christian revelation. Because the world was seen as having been created by God through his *Logos*, it could no longer be "regarded as a pale reflection of the eternal reality, as in Plato's world."[3]

[2]Andrew Louth, *Introducing Eastern Orthodoxy* (London: SPCK, 2013), 42. This use of the term *logos* to indicate not only the divine Word, incarnate in Christ, but also the inner essence or principle of each created thing, is related to the way in which Orthodoxy—unlike many Western Christian traditions—follows the Fourth Gospel in its stress that the notions of creation and redemption are strongly and intimately linked. The Western tendency to separate creation and incarnation / redemption—especially characteristic of some strands of Protestantism—is at present being challenged by some Western scholars. Nevertheless, the Orthodox "instinct"—in which the two are seen as fundamentally linked—is still rare even among these scholars.

[3]Andrew Louth, "The Cosmic Vision of Saint Maximos the Confessor,"

The early background to this particular way of focusing on the world as God's creation is a complex one, with Irenaeus' battle against Gnosticism and Athanasius' attempts to solve some of the problems of Origenist philosophy as significant factors. It is, however, in the work of the Cappadocian Fathers that we see the outline of later Orthodox thinking about creation most clearly taking shape. Here, we find that these Fathers often used the philosophical language of their day, especially that of the neoplatonic school, to articulate their theological perceptions. Indeed, as Elizabeth Theokritoff has remarked, they do this in a way that might make "the modern reader, to whom this language is alien . . . mistake their Platonic starting point for their conclusion." However, she goes on, this would be to misread their intention in using this language, which—in the context of the doctrine of creation—was to stress that it is "for the sake of the whole creation that man the microcosm receives the divine inbreathing, so that nothing in creation should be deprived of a share in communion with God." This sense of solidarity in createdness has, she goes on to note, "remained a leitmotif in Eastern Christian theology."[4]

Here, it is worthy of notice that this emphasis on solidarity in createdness has tended, in Orthodox theology, to be reflected in the distinction between Creator and creation being seen as far more important than other distinctions, such as that between natural and supernatural.[5] This tendency to stress the creator-creation distinction is in part related to Orthodoxy's refusal to make any

in Clayton and Peacocke, *In Whom We Live and Move and Have Our Being*, 188.

[4]Theokritoff, "Creator and Creation," 65.

[5]For example, angels are seen in Orthodoxy primarily as being in the same category as humans: that of created things. For the medieval West, they were primarily seen as being in a different category: part of the supernatural order, not the natural one.

separation between natural and supernatural revelation.[6] It is also in part related to the fact that, even when Orthodox writers do occasionally use the notion of some event being supernatural—in the sense of being "above nature"—this concept is understood in terms of an understanding of nature that is subtly but vitally different from that which is common in Western Christian thought. In particular, as Vladimir Lossky has noted, the Orthodox Tradition "knows nothing of 'pure nature' to which grace is added as a supernatural gift. For it, there is no natural or 'normal' state, since grace is implied in the act of creation itself."[7] The Orthodox concept of nature is such that, as we shall see presently, the concept of being "above nature" has a rather different technical meaning than that which in the West is associated with the term *supernatural.*

This Orthodox sense of the grace inherent in the created order is not, we should note, oblivious of the consequences of the fall recounted in the Book of Genesis. Indeed, as we shall see, for many patristic writers the ramifications of the fall extend beyond humanity to the entire cosmos. Yet, just as the notion of the human fall does not imply the obliteration of the image of God in humanity, so also, for Orthodoxy, the ramifications of the fallen state do not obliterate the way in which the cosmos is a revelation of the divine.

This sense of the revelation to be found in the cosmos is particularly stressed in the late fifth- or early sixth-century writings attributed to Dionysius the Areopagite. These pseudo-Dionysian writings use neoplatonic language, but it is not employed in the manner that was usual for the secular philosophy of the time.

---

[6]Such a separation is—as Dumitru Staniloae has stressed—quite alien to the Orthodox Tradition, which never makes such a separation and often—as in the work of Maximos the Confessor—seems to see the latter simply as "the historical embodiment of the former." See Staniloae, *The Experience of God,* 1.

[7]Lossky, *Mystical Theology,* 101.

Rather—as in the works of the Cappadocians—it is molded so as to make it express specifically Christian insights. While taking up the neoplatonic idea of the scale of being, the Dionysian writings turn it into what Elizabeth Theokritoff has called "a structure of *theophany*, revelation of God. Its purpose is to allow each creature to reflect the divine glory in its own unique way." In this approach, she explains, what is envisaged is "a structure in which vastly incommensurate elements—angelic, human, animate and inanimate—are all held together and function as a coherent whole, focused on their Creator. And it is a cosmos shot through with the radiance of divinity. God is at once totally other, totally beyond everything that is, and in everything by the ecstatic power inseparable from himself."[8]

This sense of God's being in all created things and yet utterly transcending them takes up an antinomy that is found at least as early as the work of St Athanasius, for whom God has no affinity with the world in his *essence*, but by his *powers* pervades the whole cosmos. This latter concept was developed by later writers in such a way that Orthodox theology has come to see, not only that God is in everything, but also that everything is in God. (This understanding is sometimes referred to as *panentheism*,[9] which, because it sees God as much more than the world, is very different from *pantheism*—the identification of God and the world—which is incompatible with Orthodox belief.)

Orthodox theology has avoided the Western tendency either to separate God from the world or else to make no proper

[8]Theokritoff, "Creator and Creation," 65–6, quoting Ps.-Dionysius, *On the Divine Names* 4.13.

[9]For a collection of essays on panentheism, see Clayton and Peacocke, *In Whom We Live and Move and Have our Being*. The Orthodox contributions to this volume—by Metropolitan Kallistos (Ware) of Diokleia, Fr Andrew Louth, Alexei Nesteruk, and myself—together provide an excellent overview of Orthodox panentheism.

distinction between them[10] in two related ways. One has been to stress the notion of the *logoi* of created things in the way that we have already noted. These *logoi*, observes Metropolitan Kallistos of Diokleia, are described by St Maximos "in two different ways, sometimes as created and sometimes as uncreated, depending upon the perspective in which they are viewed. They are created inasmuch as they inhere in the created world. But when regarded as God's presence in each thing—as divine 'predetermination' or 'preconception' concerning that thing—they are not created but uncreated."[11]

Alongside this particular panentheistic model, there exists in Orthodox teaching another, to be found in embryonic form in the writings of St Clement of Alexandria and St Basil the Great but developed most systematically in the much later work of St Gregory Palamas. This work makes a distinction between God's transcendent essence (*ousia*) and his immanent energies or operations (*energeiai*). This second approach, Metropolitan Kallistos notes, is "not contrary to the first but complementary. . . . In his essence God is infinitely transcendent, utterly beyond all created being, beyond all participation from the human side. But in his energies—which are nothing less than God himself in action—God is inexhaustibly immanent, maintaining all things

---

[10]The Orthodox panentheistic vision is very different from the view of mainstream Western Christian philosophical theism, which has tended to assume a strict separation between God and the world. In the late medieval period, the predominant Western "substance" metaphysics effectively forbade any kind of panentheism, while later attempts to move away from the resulting notion of separation tended to lead—as in the work of Spinoza—to a kind of *pantheism* in which the world and God were simply identified with one another. See the comments in Philip Clayton, "Panentheism in Metaphysical and Scientific Perspective" in Clayton and Peacocke, *In Whom We Live and Move and Have Our Being*, 75–84.

[11]Kallistos Ware, "God Immanent yet Transcendent," 160.

in being, animating them, making each of them a sacrament of his dynamic presence."[12] This panentheistic view of the relationship between the creation and its divine Creator never falls into a pantheistic identification of God with the world because the characteristic Orthodox stress on God's immanence is balanced by an equally strong stress on the utter transcendence of the divine essence, which is seen as unknowable and beyond all creaturely participation.

Over and above the implications of these two complementary models, a third factor—which we shall look at in more detail presently—prevents any descent from panentheism into pantheism in Orthodox thinking. This is that there is often, in the patristic writings, a strong sense that the world we experience only partially reflects God's ultimate intentions for his creation. The eschatological state—the "world to come"—has, they suggest, more in common with the original state for which humanity was created (the Paradise of the Genesis story) than it does with the world that we now experience as "fallen" beings. In a sense, they say, the whole cosmos now reflects the fallen human state. The "natural" world that we experience is both a revelation of God and yet also profoundly "unnatural" (or, perhaps better, "subnatural") since it reflects the fallenness of humanity and therefore does not yet manifest the fullness of God's original and ultimate intentions for his creation.

This strong Orthodox sense of the ramifications of the fall was not—as we shall note presently—always tied to an understanding of the fall as a historical event. Nevertheless, it was, as we have noted, typically expressed by the Fathers in terms of the biblical notion of the "garments of skin" given by God to fallen humans (Genesis 3.21). These were seen as referring, not just to the human body, but to "the entire postlapsarian psychosomatic

---

[12]Ware, "God Immanent Yet Transcendent," 160.

---

clothing of the human person."[13] Even for those writers who see the fallenness of the human state as in some sense affecting the whole cosmos, however, there is still a sense that each created thing is a reflection of the divine glory—a sacramental reality at least in potential.

An important aspect of St Maximos' understanding of the *logoi* of created things is one that we shall also look at in greater detail presently. This is his sense that these *logoi* should not be understood only in terms of their constituting the inner essences of those things (which we would now express, at least in part, in terms of the "laws of nature" that they obey). In addition, for Maximos, the *logoi* must be seen in terms of the ultimate end to which all created things are drawn. The *logos* of each created thing is—as Metropolitan Kallistos has put it—"God's intention for that thing, its inner essence, which makes it distinctively itself and at the same time draws it towards the divine realm."[14]

The notion that things have an intended goal (*telos* in Greek) is known as *teleology*, and this teleological aspect of God's creation has been seen by a number of scholars as central to the Orthodox understanding of creation. Vladimir Lossky, for example, has spoken of the way in which, in that understanding, the universe is seen as "dynamic . . . tending always to its final end."[15] Similarly, Fr Doru Costache has said that the Orthodox doctrine of creation "preaches the teleological conditioning of the universe."[16]

Costache makes this observation in the context of a paper in which he examines the relationship between Orthodoxy and modern scientific perceptions and rightly comments that science, "epitomized by Darwinian evolution, does not mention the

---

[13]Nellas, *Deification in Christ*, 33.

[14]Ware, "God Immanent Yet Transcendent," 160.

[15]Lossky, *Mystical Theology*, 101.

[16]Doru Costache, "The Orthodox Doctrine of Creation in the Age of Science," *Journal of Orthodox Christian Studies* 2 (2019): 62.

purposefulness of natural movement, whereas theology . . . considers teleology crucial."[17] He is, of course, correct in this observation that scientific insights arise through a methodology that precludes any mention of purpose. But what he perhaps fails to emphasize sufficiently is that the methodology of modern science *necessarily* avoids the concept of purpose,[18] and what is important is not this avoidance but the way in which at least some scientific insights are susceptible to *interpretation* in terms of purpose.

In particular, there are two such insights that are open to teleological interpretation in a way that actually clarifies an important aspect of Orthodoxy's beliefs. These are the "fine tuning" of the universe that is evident from astronomical evidence and the occurrence of "convergent evolution" in the biological world. These insights, as we shall see in the next chapter, provide a way of thinking about God's creative action that brings together naturalistic and theological perspectives in such a way as to remove the kind of tension or conflict between them that is often assumed.

---

[17]Costache, "Doctrine of Creation," 54.

[18]Modern science arose historically from the insight that the purely teleological explanations of late medieval science actually provided less insight and predictive power than explanations based on mathematical laws of nature. It is for this reason that explanations would simply cease to be "scientific" if purpose were posited as the only way to understand certain phenomena. (In practice, admittedly, certain phenomena can be understood in quasi-teleological ways, but these ways are seen simply as being a convenient kind of "shorthand" for laws that are understood in a more conventional, mathematical way.)

chapter nine

CREATION, TELEOLOGY, AND CHANCE

W e often seem, quasi-instinctively, to work with a concept of God's creation of the cosmos that has no content other than that which relates to its beginnings. We need to remember, however, that the traditional understanding of God's creative activity is far richer than this, and stresses that this activity involves sustaining everything in being and is a process of *continuous creation*. We have already noted, for example, the way in which St Basil the Great clearly anticipates a kind of evolutionary understanding in these terms, and indeed there are even deeper implications inherent in his way of thinking about the the way in which the act of creation is timeless but has continuing temporal effects. As Thomas Torrance has rightly noted, Basil sees the *fiat* of God—his "Let there be"—in terms of an understanding in which, "though acts of divine creation took place timelessly, the creative commands of God gave rise to orderly sequences and enduring structures in the world of time and space. It was thus that the voice of God in creation gave rise to laws of nature."[1]

The Western science-theology dialogue of recent years has, admittedly, largely ignored this particular patristic insight.

---

[1] Thomas F. Torrance, *The Christian Frame of Mind* (Colorado Springs: Helmers and Howard, 1989), 4.

Nevertheless, from an Orthodox perspective, it has still been very helpful in stressing an aspect of the patristic notion of continuing creation. The astonishing picture of the history of the cosmos that has been unveiled to us by the sciences can, according to most scholars involved in this dialogue, help us to develop a deeper appreciation of the way in which God's creative action occurs, not only "in the beginning," but also at all times.

If this is one of the aspects of the Western Christian response to the sciences that we Orthodox may find helpful, another that is equally helpful is that response's frequent reaction against the kind of Western natural theology that had attempted in various ways to prove God's existence through purely philosophical argument or from inference from the character of the cosmos. In part, it was this reaction that led Ian Barbour to promote an approach that was closer to the kind of natural theology that we have seen is characteristic of the mainstream Orthodox one. This approach he dubbed *theology of nature*, which he described as starting, not "from science, as some versions of natural theology do. Instead, it starts from a religious tradition based on religious experience and historical revelation. . . . Here science and religion are considered to be relatively independent sources of ideas, but with some areas of overlap in their concerns. . . . If religious beliefs are to be in harmony with scientific knowledge, some adjustments or modifications are called for."[2]

Related to Barbour's advocacy of this approach was his categorization of four ways of understanding the interaction of science and theology. First, he said, there exists among some the attitude that the two are necessarily in *conflict*. (This viewpoint is manifested by the so-called "new atheists," whose views we have noted, and also by some Protestant and Orthodox fundamentalists.) Second, Barbour explained, there is the attitude of *independence*,

[2]Ian G. Barbour, *Religion in an Age of Science*, 26.

in which it is assumed that science and theology are doing such different things—the one attempting to answer "*how*" questions and the other "*why*" questions—that the two ways of thinking simply never interact. (This is an attitude that is, as we have noted, adopted by certain Orthodox scholars. It is also to be found in certain Western theological traditions and has also been adopted by some scientists, who find it a useful rhetorical stance to keep theological opinions out of science teaching.) The third and fourth categories described by Barbour are, however, the ones that concern us here. They are what he calls *dialogue* and *integration*. Each of these, in a different way, acknowledges that there are at least some points of contact and mutual influence between science and theology.[3] They assume, as John Polkinghorne once put it, that science and theology "have important things to say to one another"[4] and, following Polkinghorne's own usage,[5] the term *dialogue* is often now used to cover all explorations based on a belief that this is the case, with many Western scholars now echoing this phraseology by speaking about *the science-theology dialogue* and pursuing the kind of theology of nature that Barbour has advocated.

[3]Barbour, *Religion in an Age of Science*, 4–30. Barbour's categorization of the two latter approaches has, admittedly, proved less than universally acceptable in its original form, since the boundary between the two categories that he delineated is not always clear, and some approaches—wherever that boundary is set—seem to manifest elements of both. But what characterized both, in Barbour's original scheme, was the belief that science and theology are neither entirely independent of each other nor necessarily in conflict.

[4]John Polkinghorne, *Scientists as Theologians: A Comparison of the Writings of Ian Barbour, Arthur Peacocke and John Polkinghorne* (London: SPCK, 1996), 3.

[5]For example, the Cambridge University paper in the Theology and Religious Studies Tripos exam that Polkinghorne oversaw until his retirement was formally called "The Modern Dialogue Between Science and Theology."

The question of what this theology of nature should consist of has not, however, always been agreed upon among those who accept its basic premise. If it is the case that, for religious beliefs to be in harmony with scientific knowledge, "some adjustments or modifications are called for," then precisely what these adjustments or modifications should be is not a matter of consensus. At one point in his own development, for example, Polkinghorne attempted to replace Barbour's distinction between dialogue and integration by speaking of a different division: between *consonance* and *assimilation*. Although Polkinghorne later replaced this division by another, it is in fact a useful one in indicating how current Western discussion does manifest certain tensions. Some, like Polkinghorne himself, seek what he then called *consonance* in the sense that they believe that science "does not determine theological thought but . . . constrains it . . . The scientific and theological accounts must fit together in a mutually consistent way."[6] Some other approaches, according to Polkinghorne, are assimilationist in that they attempt "a degree of accommodation of the one to the other that could seem to threaten [theology's] justified autonomy."[7]

Polkinghorne's attitude to the concept of God's action as Creator provides an illustration of the tension to which he points, since there are aspects of the thinking of the other two scientist-theologians on this topic that clearly worry him. Can it be right, he seems to wonder, to see this creative action—as they do—purely in terms of the naturalistic interplay between chance and the laws of nature that God has built into the world?

This questioning by Polkinghorne does not arise from any fundamental disagreement with the other two scientist-theologians about the validity of the scientist's naturalistic perspective

[6]Polkinghorne, *Scientists as Theologians*, 6f.
[7]Polkinghorne, *Scientists as Theologians*, 7.

on the development of the universe. Like them, he focuses on the immanence of God in the natural world, effectively seeing God's creative activity as being *in, with, and under* the laws of nature that the scientist can discern. In this sense he would not disagree with Peacocke's assertion that "it has become increasingly apparent that it is chance operating within a lawlike framework that is the basis of the inherent creativity of the natural order, its ability to generate new forms, patterns and organizations of matter and energy. . . . God creates in the world through what we call 'chance' operating within the created order, each stage of which constitutes the launching pad for the next."[8]

Nor is it the element of chance that seems to worry Polkinghorne, since he accepts the scientific evidence for chance having an important role in the development of the cosmos. Many religious believers have been resistant to the notion that the world is the result of the interplay of chance and physical law, since it is not immediately evident how this can be seen as consistent with the notion that the development of the cosmos has been the will of God. Nevertheless, Polkinghorne recognizes that we need to be careful here, because chance is not inconsistent with a predictable outcome. For example, the owners of gambling casinos know that even perfectly balanced roulette wheels make the the long-term profitability of their casinos highly probable. From a scientific perspective, as Polkinghorne knows, a comparable kind of long-term predictability in the cosmos may be argued for in terms of both astrophysics and evolutionary biology.

In the astrophysical arena, in particular, it has been known for several decades that the universe we live in seems to be "finely tuned" for the emergence of living beings. There are a number of "universal constants"—that which explains the strength of

---

[8]Arthur Peacocke, *Theology for a Scientific Age: Being and Becoming— Natural, Human and Divine* (London: SCM, 1993), 65, 119.

gravitational attraction for example—which do not seem to have been constrained in any naturalistic way to have the magnitude that they have. Had these been only very slightly different in value, however, they would have precluded ours from being the kind of universe in which complex life-forms could have emerged naturalistically.[9]

This kind of observation has given rise to argument about what is sometimes called the *anthropic cosmological principle*.[10] In particular, these issues have seemed to some to open the way once more to the old kind of argument from design, in which it is urged that God's existence can be proved (or at least rendered probable) by considering the cosmos's characteristics. The scientific and philosophical ramifications of this approach are, however, complex.[11] Few in the Western science-theology dialogue have taken this route even to the extent that Polkinghorne

[9]Had the strength of this gravitational constant been only very slightly lower, for example, the developmental processes which gave rise to stars— and hence to the carbon atoms which are essential to the complex molecules of which we are made—would have been impossible. On the other hand, if this constant had been only slightly greater, the universe's expansion would have ceased relatively quickly, and a collapse back into the singularity from which it emerged in the Big Bang would have taken place before these processes could be completed. In either case, only a tiny deviation from the actual value would have given rise to a situation in which living beings could not have emerged. It is not only this gravitational constant that exhibits this fine-tuning, but several others too.

[10]John D. Barrow and Frank J. Tipler, *The Anthropic Cosmological Principle* (Oxford: Clarendon, 1986) is now slightly outdated but still provides perhaps the best comprehensive review of the issues.

[11]For example, various kinds of multiple universe theories are at present popular, and it is often assumed that the existence of many universes would indicate that one universe in which conditions have been just right for the emergence of intelligent beings is unsurprising. Still, even infinite sets do not not necessarily have all possible properties. The set of odd numbers, for instance, is infinite, but no number in that set has the property of being exactly divisible by the number 2.

himself has, in his suggestion that anthropic considerations pose what he calls "a meta-question to which theism provides a persuasive (but not logically coercive) answer."[12] At the most, they have usually claimed no more than that our finely-tuned universe is consonant with the theological picture of a divine Creator who works through naturalistic processes.

In the biological sphere, a comparable view of the predictability of the interplay of chance and physical law has also recently emerged. At one time, there was widespread agreement among biologists that the termination of apparently promising evolutionary pathways indicated that the evolutionary process had no predictability. Stephen Jay Gould, for example, argued that our own presence on Earth reflects little more than a freak accident.[13] More recently, however, other biologists—the "new atheist" Richard Dawkins among them—have pointed out that certain evolutionary pathways have been followed independently on a number of occasions, so that we can see such pathways as being more likely to be taken than others.[14] In this sense, at least, the evolutionary process has a degree of predictability.

The most extreme version of this latter perspective comes from Simon Conway Morris, who has emphasized the way in which certain adaptations to particular ecological niches have happened, not only more than once but also sometimes from very different evolutionary starting points. For Morris, this underlines the notion of *evolutionary convergence*, which suggests that a number of potential evolutionary pathways may, from very different starting points, tend to converge on the same adaptive features in similar ecological environments. (The resemblances in locomotive

[12]John Polkinghorne, *Reason and Reality* (London: SPCK, 1991), 80.

[13]See for example Stephen Jay Gould, *Wonderful Life: The Burgess Shale and the Nature of History* (New York: Norton, 1989).

[14]Richard Dawkins, *The Ancestor's Tale: A Pilgrimage to the Dawn of Life* (London: Weidenfeld and Nicolson, 2004), 603–6.

features between certain marine mammals and many types of fish constitute an obvious example.) Morris even argues that, once life has begun in any part of the universe, something very like human beings as we know them are effectively bound to emerge naturalistically, though not necessarily through the kind of evolutionary pathway that our own ancestors in fact took.[15]

This last speculation may perhaps be to take the validity of the notion of evolutionary convergence too far. Nevertheless, it points us towards an important idea: that to the extent that we see the biblical notion of humans being "in the image of God" in terms of functional abilities, it is possible to see the emergence of beings created in this image as something that can be coherently thought about in terms of the evolutionary interplay of chance and the laws of nature. (The only exception to this observation may, as we have noted, be what is traditionally described as the *nous*, since it is the aspect of our mental functioning that, in Orthodox thinking, relates the human mind directly to the divine mind.)

These reflections on the effects of chance processes make it clear that we cannot simply dismiss the role of such processes in our understanding of God's creative action. As Orthodox Christians we are still likely, nevertheless, to feel that we ought to understand that action in a more subtle and theologically-nuanced way than can be provided by scientific insight alone. Might we, for example, see God, as Polkinghorne seems to, as having given a kind of freedom to creation as part of his self-emptying (*kenōsis*)? Might we also, perhaps, see God's use of chance in the way that Peacocke does, as a sort of divine "exploration" of the possibilities of the creation, analogous to the way in which a musical composer, in a fugue, explores the possibilities of a basic musical theme? (This notion may certainly have something to say for it in explaining

[15]Simon Conway Morris, *Life's Solution: Inevitable Humans in a Lonely Universe* (Cambridge: Cambridge University Press, 2003).

the extraordinary wastage and almost baroque variation that we see in the biological world.)

For many Orthodox Christians, however, there will be a sense that these pictures, even if they are valid, need to be supplemented, since they are based—at least in the context of Western assumptions about the separation of God from the world—on an understanding in which God is not seen as one who is intimately involved with its processes, since these processes are seen as being effectively autonomous. In terms of this view, God must be seen as no more than the world's designer and initiator unless there is some way in which he can "get into" the world, in later periods of time, in order to act providentially.

Within the framework of this assumption, Polkinghorne is arguably right in perceiving deistic undertones in the work of some of his Western colleagues. (The deists of the eighteenth century believed in a creator god, but saw this god's relationship with the world—after the moment of creation—as being effectively equivalent to that of an absentee landlord.) These colleagues, Polkinghorne has said, surely need to recognize examples of "Creatorly action in a more personal mode" if they are to avoid "an implicit deism . . . whose nakedness is only thinly covered by a garment of personalized metaphor."[16]

If, however, Polkinghorne's criticism is valid in terms of the presuppositions that he shares with those he criticizes, what needs to be recognized here is that these presuppositions are rooted in classic Western philosophical theism, with its notion that God and the world are separated. As we shall see in the next chapter, it is this assumption of separation that leads the great majority of participants in the Western science-theology dialogue to seek for a scientifically literate way of describing a "causal joint" between God and the world that "allows" him to act within it—if

[16]Polkinghorne, *Science and Christian Belief*, 78–9.

not in relation to his creative action, then at least in relation to other aspects of his providential action. As we have seen in our exploration of the Orthodox doctrine of creation, however, the "gap"[17] that is presupposed by these Western scholars is simply not a part of our Orthodox understanding. It is for this reason that for Orthodoxy—as we shall see—the "problem" of divine action that is perceived by these scholars simply does not exist.

[17]This gap is not, we should perhaps note here, the kind of gap presupposed in the notion of the "God of the gaps" that has been criticized within the Western science-theology dialogue. Nevertheless, as we shall see in the next chapter, the two kinds of gap are not unrelated.

chapter ten

COUNTERING COMMON
DISTORTIONS

We Christians—whether of the East or the West—are faced with a complex task in trying to answer the question of how we should respond to the insights of modern science. We can only undertake this task adequately if, in addition to understanding the well-established theories of modern science and exploring the relevance of the theological traditions that inform our thinking, we also recognize the influence on us of the intellectual climate in which we live, which inevitably affects the kinds of questions that we ask.

This is particularly important in the Orthodox world. We usually now believe that around the middle of the twentieth century our Orthodox theology—through the "neo-patristic" movement—finally escaped from its reliance on those Western Christian philosophical and theological frameworks which had, up to that period, strongly influenced our theological thinking for several centuries. This perception of our recent history is, it must be said, largely valid, and there can be no doubt that the scholars who led this attempt to escape our "Babylonian captivity" have performed an extremely important task. [1] On the other hand, not

[1]This escape—begun in nineteenth century Russia—happened largely through the twentieth-century "neo-patristic" work of Russian scholars resident in the West, such as Georges Florovsky and Vladimir Lossky. A little

only has this movement's stress on a return to the Fathers often had the (unintended) effect of making some of us look solely to the past in a way that makes it difficult to face the challenges of the present,[2] but in addition—and more importantly—the genuine successes of the movement have led us to believe that the task that was undertaken has now been largely completed. But in relation to our understanding of our doctrine of creation, it has—at least in my judgment—hardly begun.

What I mean by this is that, in certain important respects, the implicit assumptions that are often brought to our understanding of creation still reflect Western suppositions of the sort that lead Western scholars to assume a separation between God and the world. These assumptions are the result of Western Christian developments that, while incompatible with Orthodoxy, have been instrumental in forming an implicit conceptual framework that affects not only Western Christians but Orthodox ones too. In this chapter, therefore, we shall examine the history of these developments and explore the reasons that they represent a distortion of how science should be viewed from the perspective of the Christian faith.

In origin, the word *science* simply means knowledge. It has only been since the early nineteenth century that the term *scientist* has come, in English, to mean the person who pursues the particular kind of knowledge that arises solely from what we now think of as a "scientific" kind of methodology. Prior to this, those we now think of as scientists often referred to themselves as *natural philosophers*, and the borderline between what we now call science and other kinds of knowing was less well-defined than it has since seemed to become.

later, in the second half of the century, Greek scholars like Christos Yannaras and John Zizioulas made comparable contributions.

[2]Pantelis Kalaitzidis, "Challenges of Renewal and Reformation Facing the Orthodox Church," *Ecumenical Review* 61 (2009): 136–164.

A problem for us here is that the way science is now taught—both at elementary and advanced levels—is aimed at producing effective technicians or scientific researchers rather than people who can reflect philosophically on their vocations. This teaching rarely does justice either to the historical complexity of scientific activity or to the current range of philosophical understandings of that activity. A full knowledge of these factors points us, not towards some well-defined methodology that characterizes science, but rather to a range of related methodologies that change with time and, in any given period, vary somewhat from discipline to discipline. Because of the gaps in their general education, however, many (indeed most) working scientists tend to make assumptions about the character and scope of science that—as philosophers and historians of science often point out—are only partially justifiable.

Even when historical and philosophical complexities are taken into account, however, it is still possible to see important links between the methodologies of present and past scientists and to talk at least broadly about the scientific approach to understanding the world. Since the dawn of humanity, the human rational faculty has been used to try to make sense of observational data. The astronomical alignments of some of the megalithic monuments of north-west Europe indicate that systematic collection of such data probably goes back for thousands of years, and certainly, by the time of the ancient Greeks who lived around half a millennium before the Christian era, observational evidence was collected systematically and used in a remarkably sophisticated way. This early Greek science was passed on, through Eastern Christian communities, to the Islamic world.[3] In that world—with important borrowings from Indian mathematics—it was refined

[3]See De Lacey O'Leary, *How Greek Science Passed to the Arabs* (London: Routledge and Kegan Paul, 1949).

and improved before being transmitted, in the medieval period, to those Western Europeans who, with an increasing emphasis on experiment, paved the way for science in its modern forms.

Even taking into account the sophistication of ancient and medieval science, it remains true, by and large, that it was in Western Europe—especially from the mid-seventeenth century onwards—that scientific methodologies as we now know them came to maturity. Some historians have seen the Christian understanding of the rationality of God's creation as an important factor in this development,[4] and certainly there was often, for scientists of the early modern period, an explicitly Christian underpinning to their justification for their methods.

Despite this, a few modern authors have seen the development of early modern science as something essentially anti-Christian: a move away from the direct contemplation of the created world and towards a de-sacralized view of the world, in which—to use the term adopted by the early scientific pioneer, Roger Bacon—the cosmos needs to be "tortured" to reveal its secrets. (In the Orthodox world this view has been expressed by Philip Sherrard.[5]) Yet as the historian, Peter Harrison, has emphasized,[6] there was, in this early modern period, much discussion of the justification for the scientific approach, and not infrequently this was based on explicit theological arguments. In particular, it was argued that the fall had rendered inoperative the direct contemplative knowledge of the cosmos that had existed in unfallen humanity. From an Orthodox perspective, this attempt at justification

[4]This is a view particularly associated with Stanley Jaki; see, e.g., his work, *The Origin of Science and the Science of Its Origins* (Edinburgh: Scottish Academic Press, 1978).

[5]See, e.g., Philip Sherrard, "Modern Science and the Dehumanization of Man," *Studies in Comparative Religion* 10 (1976).

[6]Peter Harrison, *The Fall of Man and the Foundations of Science* (Cambridge: Cambridge University Press, 2007).

can be criticized, since it has its roots in a Western Augustinian view of the fall that does not correspond to Orthodox thinking. Nevertheless, to see the epistemological foundations of science as involving a move away from Christian commitment is extremely simplistic. The majority of scientists in this period were devout Christian believers, who perceived their work as bringing into view something of the thought and will of the divine Creator.

By the mid-eighteenth century this situation had begun to change. In particular, critical, rational assessment of evidence was now proving so fruitful when applied to the natural world that it was inevitably applied also to other domains of human reflection. In relation to the Bible, for instance, a problem arose for some because the subtle, traditional kind of scriptural interpretation that had been characteristic of Christian understanding in the late antique and medieval periods had largely been lost to view.[7] When people like Voltaire pointed out the problems of the kind of literalist reading of Scripture that was by this time predominant among Western Christians, it often seemed—both to the attackers and those attacked—that what was being challenged was nothing less than Christianity itself. Questions about *rationality*—the catchword of this "Enlightenment" period—thus became a problem for some Christians, even if at this stage the problem lay not so much in the content of what we now call

[7]In the *Philokalia*—not the modern *Philokalia* but an anthology of the works of Origen edited by St Basil the Great and St Gregory Nazianzen (and purged of the more questionable elements of Origen's thought)—there had been a division of Scripture into three levels of meaning: the literal, the moral, and the spiritual. There was a clear understanding that on occasion it was proper for the literal meaning to be set aside. In the West, however, the Reformation had involved a Protestant rejection of the kind of allegorical interpretation that had previously been the norm, and this evoked a response in the Roman Catholic "counter-reformation" in which, although this traditional mode of interpretation was not rejected entirely, a new literalism tended to prevail in much the same way as in Protestantism.

science as in its underlying approach to the question of how truth was to be perceived. Increasingly, there was an apparent tension between what were seen as "rational" understanding and "blind" religious faith.

In this period, however, "rational" attacks on traditional forms of Christianity were only rarely atheistic ones. It was still widely assumed that a rational religious faith was possible, and usually these attacks involved, at most, what was called *deism*: a view that defended the appropriateness of speaking of a divine Creator, but which tended to assume that this Creator was to be known purely through philosophical insight rather than through spiritual experience or through divine revelation in historical acts. Observations that had appeared in the early decades of the new science, in books such as John Ray's *The Wisdom of God in the Works of Creation* (1691), were now, in studies like William Paley's *Natural Theology* (1802), recast in a more clearly rationalist form. God's existence, it was now claimed, could be known logically through the apparent "design" of the world.

In addition to challenging the older notion that God was to be known primarily through religious experience and through revelation in historical acts, the deists also tended to reject any notion of the miraculous. Here, science—once again, not so much in its content as in the world-view it was perceived as promoting—was clearly a factor. At one time, events like earthquakes and lightning strikes had been widely seen as supernatural acts of God. By the eighteenth century, however, such events were coming to be seen as the outcome of the regularities of the world—the "laws of nature"—and it seemed to many that most events that had hitherto been seen as examples of God's "special," direct action would come to be understood in a naturalistic way. Indeed, some, like the philosopher David Hume, went further. They argued that, even if there seemed to be strong anecdotal evidence for events that seemed at odds with the known laws of nature, we should see this evidence as less weighty than the evidence that all events do in fact obey natural laws. Thus, they argued, there is good reason to argue that miracles do not occur.

A full-blown deism, however, which denied the miraculous, was never in this period the position of more than a small minority in the West. What was far more common was an approach that remained more distinctly Christian but was affected in some degree by the factors that had been significant for deistic thinking. Thus, for example, the Western medieval notion of the supernatural—in which grace had been seen as "completing" nature—was now widely used in a less subtle way than it had been. In particular, the separation of grace and nature that had characterized this approach (and that went back to the thinking of St Augustine of Hippo) was now even more strongly emphasized. On supposedly scientific grounds, nature was now widely seen as a kind of clockwork mechanism, and consequently grace was simplistically identified with events that were not capable of scientific explanation.[8] If there was a *gap* in scientific explanation, it was assumed that this was where God could be seen at work.

In this way, what has been called the *God-of-the-gaps* understanding of divine action became widespread. For those who accepted the historical evidence for miracles, the scriptural and anecdotal witness to these miracles was seen as indicating a significant gap in understanding that pointed to the reality of God. And both for the deists, who denied the occurrence of miracles, and for more conservative Western Christians, who believed in them, the apparent design of the world was seen as a "gap" that

[8]This Western belief in an essentially autonomous universe was not entirely new in this period, but was based in part on assumptions that went back to the scholasticism of the late medieval period and even, in some respects, to an Augustinian separation between grace and nature, which had affected Western theology in numerous ways.

could provide a powerful argument for the reality of God as Creator of the cosmos.

The intricate interconnectedness of the components of the empirical world now became the basis of an "argument from design" that could, it was believed, be used to prove God's reality. If you found a watch and examined its elaborate mechanism, Paley argued, then—even if you didn't know the watch's purpose—you would necessarily conclude that it was the product of a purposeful and intelligent designer. In a comparable way, he argued, the intricacy of the natural world could also be seen as pointing clearly to its purposeful and intelligent design.

This kind of argument became, for some Western Christians, almost the main underpinning for religious belief. By the early nineteenth century, even those who were far from being deists, in the strict sense of the term, often had views that relied in part on "proof" arguments of this kind. It was because of this that the evolutionary theory of Charles Darwin came to be seen by many of them as a major threat.

While some saw the new theory as a challenge to their literalist reading of the creation accounts in Genesis, this was not the only or even the main issue that presented itself. Some had already started to read these accounts in a more nuanced way, not least because of geological evidence of the great age of the Earth. These were happy to interpret the "days" of creation as æons of indeterminate length, but they were still often troubled by Darwin's insights into natural selection, since they saw each "day" as representing a new, "special" act of God. A gap in scientific explanation—which by virtue of being a gap had seemed to provide a major apologetic argument in favor of God's existence—had now, it was claimed, been filled by science.[9]

[9]The point here was that the apparent design of the world—the interrelationship of its parts and the particular attributes of each species—could

In the decades immediately after the publication of Darwin's theory, it was by no means obvious that this theory was valid, since there were still scientific issues that required careful examination. Though Darwin's achievement was a magnificent one, it was only later, through the integration of genetic insights unknown to Darwin himself, that his evolutionary theory could be regarded as robust from a scientific perspective. This sense of the robustness of the evolutionary scenario was reinforced later still by insights into the chemical processes involved, with the discovery of the structure of DNA being a key development. The scientific consensus about evolution that now exists is based, therefore, not only on Darwin's own arguments, but on the whole of what is usually called the *Neo-Darwinian synthesis*. By incorporating genetic insights and refining Darwin's own views, this synthesis has done away with any scientific weaknesses that those views may have had in their original form.

Nevertheless, as we have noted, there are still some Christians who ignore all this cumulative evidence, their motivation usually being based on a kind of fundamentalism, often in relation to the Bible, but sometimes—in its Orthodox version—in relation to the views of some of the Church Fathers. These fundamentalists sometimes seem to believe that they can sustain their rejection of the evolutionary scenario through scientific argument.

now be seen for the first time as the result of the "natural selection" of minor modifications that had occurred in the normal process of variation between parents and offspring. Those fittest to survive to produce a new generation of offspring would do so more often than their unmodified counterparts, and the cumulative effects of change would eventually give rise to new species. In practice, this Darwinian understanding has, since Darwin's time, been developed in a number of ways (some, for example, stressing the possible importance of variations that are not minor). Nevertheless, the notion of evolution through natural selection as an explanation of the apparent "design" of the world has not only survived, but has become the bedrock of modern biological understanding.

A few, for example, effectively ignore the Neo-Darwinian synthesis in its current form and focus on the way in which Darwin's own evidence and reasoning were less conclusive than he himself believed. In the light of the current synthesis, however, most Christians who feel the need to challenge evolutionary theory have moved beyond this anachronistic kind of criticism, and have recognized that a critique of current Neo-Darwinism is now necessary if it is to give the impression of being scientifically well-informed.

The main attempt to develop such a critique has been through the concept of "Intelligent Design" (ID), which asserts that certain aspects of the created order manifest an "irreducible complexity" that could not have come about through a process of natural selection through random mutation. In its earlier and more simplistic forms, this ID movement's supporters tended to rely on arguments about things like eyes and wings. Without design, they asked, how could the complexity of the eye possibly have evolved gradually from something simpler? What, they asked rhetorically, could be the advantage of a sort of half-eye? How could feathers have come about, they asked, when you can't have flight without them, but without flight there would be no evolutionary advantage to having feathers?

Evolutionary biologists did not find it hard, however, to point out that there would clearly have been selective advantage in the kind of simpler light-detecting organ from which a more complex eye evolved, and that feathers would have had an advantage in providing thermal insulation long before they took on a role in flight. The proponents of ID had to work harder than they had, therefore, to attempt to sustain their kind of objection, and in due course came up with more complex arguments involving abstruse details of certain organisms, such as the flagella of certain bacteria.

In no case, however, have biologists in general—religious believers included—found these arguments convincing. In fact, they have in all cases answered these challenges with at least a plausible evolutionary scenario, making the important point that (as in the case of feathers) the current functional role of any characteristic of a particular species does not need to be the same as that which gave a selective advantage to that species' distant ancestors, in which that characteristic originally evolved.

It is important to recognize, not only that the scientific validity of ID arguments is highly questionable, but also that much of the motivation for pursuing such argument is a "God of the gaps" understanding that is theologically questionable. Not only have any gaps pointed out by proponents of ID proved, sooner or later, to be susceptible to being filled through scientific understanding, but more importantly, there is a basic theological flaw in any understanding based on supposed "gaps" in scientific understanding. This flaw is a failure to recognize the traditional Christian emphasis—still central to Orthodox understanding—on God's immanence in creation, and the way in which God should be seen as present and active in all natural processes.

Even in the immediate aftermath of the Darwinian revolution in biology, this essential insight was highlighted by at least some scholars. The Anglican priest, Aubrey Moore, for example, in a book published in 1889, pointed out the theological implications of the (then common) "special creation" interpretation of the Genesis accounts, in which the world is interpreted as the outcome of a series of "special" divine creative acts. The Darwinian view, he argued, should be seen as "infinitely more Christian than the theory of 'special creation.' For it implies the immanence of God in nature, and the omnipresence of his creative power." Those, he went on, "who oppose the doctrine of evolution in defense of a 'continued intervention' of God seem to have failed to notice that a theory of occasional intervention implies as its correlative a theory of ordinary absence."[10]

Because of the way in which the thought of the Enlightenment period had exacerbated Western Christians' tendency to separate grace and nature, the "ordinary absence" of God that Moore challenged was something that many of them seem effectively to have assumed. And in several ways it is against this "ordinary absence" that many participants in the recent Western science-theology dialogue have reacted in recent decades, stressing the immanence of God in creation in a way that Orthodox Christians can certainly applaud as a move in the right direction.

Even so, we should not underestimate the continuing effects of the kind of quasi-deistic thinking that tends to lead to God's immanence in creation being underemphasized or even ignored, so that God is at least implicitly viewed as a kind of absentee landlord who occasionally visits the tenants. This essentially deitic, sub-Christian picture is, even among Orthodox, a common and easily-adopted assumption in a scientific age. If only unconsciously, many Christians have been influenced by the sort of mental picture—supposedly "scientific"—in which God is no more than the "God of the gaps," the created world being seen as a kind of clockwork mechanism which, once "wound up," runs on its own until God makes one of his occasional interventions.

This mental picture—essentially Paley's notion of the world as analogous to a watch—is theologically dangerous, and not only because it is associated with "proof of God's existence" arguments that have now been rendered impotent by the notion of evolution as the "blind watchmaker."[11] It is dangerous also because it

[10]A. L. Moore, *Science and Faith* (London: Kegan Paul, Trench and Co., 1889), 184.

[11]See Richard Dawkins, *The Blind Watchmaker* (London: Longman, 1986) for an excellent (though occasionally explicitly atheistic) explanation

can easily undermine something that Orthodox Christianity sees as essential, since it is intrinsic to both the notion of the *logoi* of created things expounded by St Maximos the Confessor and the doctrine of the divine energies articulated by St Gregory Palamas. This is that the cosmos is infused by God's presence—a presence without which it could not exist at all, since it is utterly, and in all its parts, upheld in being by God from moment to moment.

But if something akin to this Orthodox sense of the immanence of God in creation has often been stressed in recent years by Western scholars, it would seem that they have often failed to recognize fully the way in which their way of posing questions is still influenced by the quasi-deistic view that they claim to have rejected. In particular, as we shall see, they still tend to approach the issue of God's action in the world by seeing it in terms of the "problem" of how God can act in a world characterized by obedience to "laws of nature." The problem, as they see it, is one of identification of the point of interaction—the "causal joint"—that enables God to work in a created order characterized by essentially autonomous natural processes, and various possibilities have been suggested as at least scientifically plausible.

Here, speaking of the way in which the cosmos obeys "laws of nature" has led them to make, at least implicitly, comparisons with other "lawlike" mechanisms that are, from an Orthodox perspective, disastrously misleading. If they have (rightly) abandoned Paley's watchmaker analogy in favor of the "blind watchmaker" of evolution, they have still, as we shall see, retained a distinction between God and the created order that has in it something of Paley's sense of the relationship between the watchmaker and the watch.[12]

of the biological understanding of why the "design" argument for God is no longer tenable in the form set out by Paley.

[12]This implicit gap is still present in the thinking of people who believe they have avoided any such gap by adopting some kind of *panentheism*

It is in terms of this background that we can understand the way in which divine action is usually approached within the Western science-theology dialogue. This Western approach is based on a conceptual framework—quite different from our Orthodox one—in which God is separated from his creation. If the "God of the gaps" has been rejected, a different kind of gap between God and the world is still assumed.

It is this Western "separation" notion that leads to the belief that the defense of "traditional" Christian beliefs requires acknowledgment of two modes of divine action: the "general" kind that involves simply the normal working of the laws of nature, and the "special" kind that arises when God *responds* to events in the world, either through setting aside the laws of nature and intervening supernaturally, or else through manipulating those laws through some kind of "causal joint." This Western picture of two essentially separate modes of divine action—sustaining the world in being and manipulating it—is, we should note, based on a picture of God that is questionable from an Orthodox perspective, not only because of its roots in a Western "separation" model, but in two other ways.

First, it involves a notion of God as a *temporal* being. God is seen, in events of "special" divine action, as *responding* to events in the world much as any other temporal agent must. The traditional notion of God's eternal and timeless being is effectively ignored.

(defined by the notion that the world is not separated from God but is, in some sense, "in God"). As we shall see, theirs is in fact only what we might call a *weak panentheism*. They still, in their belief in a "causal joint" between God and the cosmos, implicitly suppose that there is a gap between the two that needs to be bridged if certain events are to be explained in terms of "special" divine action. By contrast, Orthodoxy—despite its strong stress on making a proper distinction between the created and the uncreated—does not perceive any such gap because it presupposes, as we shall see, a more radical kind of panentheism than theirs.

(This traditional notion is, we should note, now reinforced for us by relativity theory's demonstration that time is part of the created order and not something within which creation unfolds. Our Orthodox emphasis on the distinction between Creator and creation thus underlines for us the way in which God should not be seen as a temporal being, but as eternal in the way that was generally understood within both Eastern and Western Christian theologies before the early modern period.[13])

The second oversimplification in this scheme is to regard God as one who acts in a way that is comparable to the way in which a created agent does: as a time-bound "person." There is little or no sense that speaking about God as personal should be understood in an apophatic way, nor is there any sense of God as a Trinity of persons, whose action is "from the Father, through the Son, and in (or by) the Holy Spirit." (We shall return to this Trinitarian point presently.)

It is not only in terms such as these, however, that the causal joint scheme for understanding divine action is questionable. Even when looked at it its own terms, this model proves to be so problematic that—as Nicholas Saunders has said in his classic examination of the topic—contemporary Western theology "*is*

---

[13]This classical notion of divine eternity is still influential within the Roman Catholic world, so that it is notable that the temporal scheme at the heart of the "causal joint" model seems to have less influence among Roman Catholic participants in the science-theology dialogue than among their Protestant colleagues. Many of these Roman Catholics, as a result, still look at divine action in terms of scholastic distinction between primary and secondary causes. Quite rightly, one Western critic of the causal joint approach to divine action has noted that it is based on an ignorance or rejection of traditional perspectives, being a manifestation of "theism of the modern kind . . . a distinctively Protestant deviation from the mainstream classical view." See Wesley Wildman, "Robert John Russell's Theology of God's Action," in Ted Peters and Nathan Hallanger, eds., *God's Action in the World: Essays in Honour of Robert John Russell* (Aldershot: Ashgate, 2006), 166.

in a crisis."[14] Moreover, the kind of *impasse* in which, according to Saunders, the supporters of the causal joint scheme find themselves is based on a judgment that has its roots in an inadequate conceptual scheme. For if contemporary Western theology is indeed in a crisis in its exploration of divine action, this crisis is not just due to the difficulty of finding a coherent causal joint model for "special" acts of God. The problem lies also in the inadequacy of the underlying assumption of the essentially autonomous character of the natural world, which leads to the belief that acts of this kind are necessary.

Some Western scholars have, we should perhaps note, tried to address some of the problems of this causal joint approach by adopting a strategy that they label as *panentheism*. This term is defined by the belief that God and the world are not separated in the way that Western philosophical theism has usually held. Rather, the world is seen as being in some sense "in God." As we have seen in our exploration of the Orthodox doctrine of creation, we Orthodox Christians do have a view that is panentheistic in this general sense, so that it might seem, at first sight, that some kind of causal joint view, when allied to a panentheistic framework, might be acceptable to us. In practice, however, panentheism is not used by these Western scholars as it is in the Orthodox world: as something that arises from fundamental theological insights. Rather, it is used (unsuccessfully) to attempt to deal with some of the problems associated with the causal joint model that they share with those who reject their panentheism.[15]

[14]Nicholas Saunders, *Divine Action and Modern Science* (Cambridge: Cambridge University Press, 2002), 215. A deeper philosophical analysis of the shortcomings of the scheme has more recently been articulated in Sarah Lane Ritchie, *Divine Action and the Human Mind* (Cambridge: Cambridge University Press, 2019).

[15]The understanding of the anti-panentheist John Polkinghorne, for example, is essentially no different from that of panentheists such as Philip

Part of the problem here is that the concept of panentheism tends to be defined by these Western scholars in purely negative terms: as a rejection of the notion—characteristic of traditional Western philosophical theism—that God and the world are totally separated. Usually, in trying to explain what it is to be "in" God, recourse is had to some rather vague analogy, such as the relationship between the the mind and the body, or between a fetus and its mother. In terms of these analogies, panentheism is in fact a position that takes many forms, some of which are mutually exclusive. We need, therefore, to be aware of this range of possible meanings, and to recognize that, in its Orthodox form, panentheism is far more than simply the notion that the world is "in God." Orthodox panentheism arises, not from a simple definition or analogy, but—as we have seen—from a subtle and profound theology of creation.

Having said all this, however, a question remains. It is that of whether—given that divine action is not a "problem" for Orthodoxy in the way that it is in the West—we can actually develop an understanding of divine action that can be persuasive in the light of modern science. In relation to this question, I have proposed that we can in fact construct what I have called a *neo-Byzantine model* of divine action,[16] based in part on those aspects of St Maximos' thinking that we have already examined, and in part on what may at first seem a rather unlikely source of insight. This

Clayton and Arthur Peacocke. All three still advocate an understanding of "special" divine action based on causal joint processes. See the discussion in Christopher C. Knight, "Theistic Naturalism and the Word Made Flesh: Complementary Approaches to the Debate on Panentheism," in Clayton and Peacocke, *In Whom We Live and Move*, 48–61.

[16]This model was first presented in Christopher C. Knight, "Divine Action: A Neo-Byzantine Model," *International Journal for Philosophy of Religion* 58 (2005): 181–199, and is discussed in detail in Christopher C. Knight, *The God of Nature.*

second source of insight is our Orthodox understanding of the fall. It is to this, therefore, that we must now turn, since it proves to be a major theological resource for thinking about the character of the "natural" world and, by extension, for thinking about how God acts within that world.

chapter eleven

GARMENTS OF SKIN

From an Orthodox point of view, the mainstream theological thinking of the West has rarely, if ever, properly acknowledged the radical difference between the world of our everyday experience and the world as it is in God's ultimate intention for it. We Orthodox tend to express this ultimate intention, not only by looking forward to the eschatological state—the "new creation" spoken of in the New Testament—but also by looking backwards to the Paradise from which, according to the Genesis story, our first ancestors were expelled. This story, according to Orthodox understanding, indicates that God's "original" world has had to be radically modified by him because of the rebellion of his creatures. Indeed, in a theological sense—though not in the philosophical sense in which the term "natural" is usually used—we should see the empirical world in which we live as "unnatural" or—perhaps better—"subnatural."

Philip Sherrard has expressed the contrast between Eastern and Western Christian perceptions of "nature" in terms of the different understandings of the resurrection of the dead to be found in writers of the early centuries of the Christian faith. In the West, he notes, there was in this period a strong stress—as in Tertullian—on the resurrection of the "flesh," by which was meant quite explicitly the flesh of the body experienced in our earthly life. In the East, by contrast, there was an alternative understanding, especially in writers such as St Gregory of Nyssa and St Maximos the Confessor. In this latter understanding, says Sherrard, the resurrection body was not identified with the body in its present state, "composed of juices and glands and organs for excreting and procreating, and subject to the processes of conception, childbirth, adulthood, old age, sickness, and death." These aspects of the earthly body were not seen as parts of the "original" body intended by God when he created the world. Rather, using an allegorical interpretation of Genesis 3.21 that was widely used in the Christian East, these characteristics of the earthly body were seen as "aspects of the 'garments of skin' added to the original body as a result of the fall. They are as it were accretions, things grown over the body."[1]

In using this concept of *garments of skin*, patristic writers were not simply, we should note, developing a theological model on the basis of the kind of allegorical biblical interpretation that might seem somewhat arbitrary. They were, in fact, using this notion as a kind of shorthand for a more general and easily accepted biblical insight. For, according to this patristic perspective, the distinctions between the pre- and post-fall condition of humankind (as outlined in the Book of Genesis) and between this world and the "new creation" (to be found in various parts of the New Testament) are such that we must be extremely careful in using our experience of the present world as a guide to God's original or ultimate intentions for his creation. Western Christian theology tends to err in its reflection on creation, according to this viewpoint, precisely because it fails to recognize the reality to which the notion of "garments of skin" points.

The importance of this divergence between East and West is by no means limited to the particular issues on which Sherrard

---

[1]Philip Sherrard, *Christianity and Eros: Essays on the Theme of Sexual Love* (London: SPCK, 1976), 40.

himself focuses.[2] His perception that Western Christian reflection on the world makes "no sharp distinction . . . between the order of nature prior to the fall and the order of nature subsequent to the fall"[3] is one that has many ramifications. In particular, if we come to accept the validity of his view that the world as we know it "is not that which God has created or intended for man, but is what man has brought on himself as a result of his own defection and error,"[4] this perception will affect our theological framework in numerous ways. Its acceptance will not simply allow us to move beyond Western theology's tendency to see the biblical concept of the fall as having implications only for humanity rather than for the entire cosmos. It will also provide us with an important resource for the resolution of two major problems faced by theologians in the West: that which is usually called the problem of evil, and that of how God may be said to act in the world.

The first of these problems arises when our conception of God—in which he is understood to be omnipotent and wholly good—is coupled with the observation that evil exists. For, as many have noted, there seems to be an inherent contradiction in this combination.[5] One aspect of this is, admittedly, less difficult to deal with than the other, since, when faced with the question of why God allows "human" evil, Christians tend to be convinced by the argument that human free-will is so central to the divine purpose that its hindrance can only rarely if ever be appropriate. When it comes to the problem of "natural" evil, however, most

[2]This is the issue of human sexuality. For a discussion of Sherrard's approach, see Christopher C. Knight, "Natural Law and the Problem of Contraception: Some Neglected Perspectives," *New Blackfriars* 87 (2006): 505ff., in which it is argued that some of Sherrard's views may, in this particular context, require expansion from a scientific perspective.

[3]Sherrard, *Christianity and Eros*, 25.

[4]Sherrard, *Christianity and Eros,* 26.

[5]See, e.g., J. L. Mackie, "Evil and Omnipotence," in B. Mitchell, ed., *The Philosophy of Religion* (Oxford: Oxford University Press, 1971), 92f.

Christians are usually less sure in their response. Faced with some of the less palatable consequences of the "laws of nature"—the child drowned by a tsunami, for example—they cannot help feeling uneasy. They may recognize that rational choice is only possible against a background of regularity of a kind that the laws of nature provide.[6] Nevertheless, they cannot help feeling that a created order that God saw as "good" (Genesis 1.25) should be more uniformly benign.

For some, an answer to this problem lies in the occasional biblical hints about the universe being, in some sense, under the sway of "principalities and powers" that are hostile or indifferent to God's ultimate intentions (Eph 6.12; Col 2.15). For many, however, this concept has seemed difficult to incorporate into their wider theological understanding, both because of its non-scientific imagery and because it has seemed to contradict the notion that God made the world and saw that it was good. It is arguable, nevertheless, that this "principalities and powers" notion is of considerable consequence,[7] for it points towards an important aspect of the tension inherent in speaking about the empirical world as God's creation.

Put in biblical imagery, this tension might be expressed as follows: On the one hand, we want, with the psalmist, to see the lion stalking its prey as seeking its food "from God" (Ps 103/4.21). On the other hand, we also want to say, with the Book of Isaiah, that when God's ultimate purposes are fulfilled, "the wolf shall dwell with the lamb and the leopard shall lie down with the kid" (Is 11.6). And in wanting to use both of these images, we are implicitly admitting to an ambiguity in our attitude to God's creation as

[6]This view can be found, for example, in F. R. Tennant, *Philosophical Theology* (Cambridge: Cambridge University Press, 1930).

[7]For an interesting study of this by an Orthodox author, see David Bentley Hart, *The Doors of the Sea: Where Was God in the Tsunami?* (Grand Rapids: Eerdmans, 2005).

we experience it. We want to say both that this is God's world and yet that it is not *fully* that world as God ultimately intends it to be. And as the animal imagery indicates, the problem of evil—at least as the carnivorous hunter's prey might perceive it—is an important aspect of this tension.

At this point, Western philosophical approaches to the problem of evil fail to go far enough. They may be correct, for example, when they suggest that human life and choice are only possible against a background of regularity that necessarily has unwanted effects. They may also be correct—as St Irenaeus' thought suggests—that evil is a necessary aspect of a world that is a "vale of soul-making."[8] In their different ways, however, such approaches assume that our understanding of the link between this world and the "new creation" can be developed only in terms of the question of how the problematic aspects of the former may be seen as necessary to provide conditions through which the latter may be attained. God's will can in some sense, it is assumed, encompass the evil in the world because a greater good is derived from that evil.

While this is little more than an assertion for Western theological approaches, however, the Orthodox Tradition has resources here that Western traditions have, at best, only in a diluted form. This can be seen by a careful study of what is perhaps the best modern summary of this aspect of the Eastern tradition—Panayiotis Nellas' book, *Deification in Christ*—which begins by stressing the way in which man is seen, biblically, as having been made in the image of God (Gen 1.26). This notion, says Nellas, provides for patristic writers the basis for a perspective in which "the essence of man is not found in the matter from which he was

[8] An interesting analysis of this "vale of soul making" idea is to be found in John Hick, *Evil and the God of Love* (London: Collins, 1966).

created but in the archetype on the basis of which he was formed and towards which he tends."[9]

This belief that the ontology of man is to be found, not in matter, but in the image in which he is created, does not, Nellas stresses, mean that we should interpret this patristic picture in simple dualistic terms, in which it is the soul that is created in the image of God. Rather, he says, this belief is based on the perception that the "ontological truth of man does not lie in himself conceived as an autonomous being—in his natural characteristics, as materialist theories maintain; in the soul or in the intellect . . . as many ancient philosophers believed; or exclusively in the person of man, as contemporary philosophical systems centered on the person accept. No: it lies in the Archetype. Since man is an image, his real *being* is not defined by the created element with which the image is constructed. . . . Man is understood ontologically by the Fathers only as a theological being. His ontology is iconic."[10]

What, then, is this "archetype" that Nellas sees as so central to Eastern patristic thought? Fundamentally, he says, the key lies in the prologue of the fourth gospel (Jn 1.1–14): "the archetype is Christ"[11]—not simply as the *Logos* of God, but more specifically as the *incarnate Logos*.[12] This stress on incarnation is, for Nellas, as applicable before the historical incarnation in Jesus as after, since, on the level of the "supra-temporal reality of God" Christ must be seen as "the first born of all creation" (Col 1.15–17) and not as "a mere event or happening in history."[13] Even before the fall, says Nellas (reflecting a view found in St Irenaeus and others) man had "need of salvation, since he was an imperfect and

[9]Nellas, *Deification in Christ,* 33.
[10]Nellas, *Deification in Christ,* 33f.
[11]Nellas, *Deification in Christ,* 34.
[12]Nellas, *Deification in Christ,* 35, quoting Nicolas Cabasilas, *The Life in Christ* (PG 150:681AB).
[13]Nellas, *Deification in Christ,* 35.

incomplete 'child.' "[14] Christ accomplishes man's salvation "not only in a negative way, liberating him from the consequences of original sin, but also in a positive way, completing his iconic, prelapsarian 'being.' "[15]

In this perspective, Nellas continues, the history of human-kind—and indeed of the whole universe—can only partially be understood in terms of secular disciplines. "Since the ontological origin of man is not to be found in his biological being but in his being in Christ, and the realization of his being in Christ consti-tutes a journey from the . . . iconic to that which truly exists, his-tory can be understood precisely as the realization of this journey. As such, it has its beginning and its end in Christ." Reflecting the notion of the cosmic Christ to be found in the biblical letters to the Ephesians and Colossians, the patristic writers insist that it is "not only the present and the past which move and determine history but also . . . the advent, at the end of the age, of Christ the recapitulator of all things, that is, of the Logos together with his body, the transformed world."[16]

This perspective, Nellas continues, implies that "the devel-opment or evolution of humanity is illuminated inwardly. Our understanding of humanity is not determined simply by the pro-cesses of change which are observed in the matter of the image, but, without this first aspect being overlooked, our viewpoint is extended and understood primarily in terms of an evolution or raising up of the image to the Archetype. . . . Evolution in this way is understood in all its dimensions—not only in those which are determined by scientific observation—and is given its true and full value."[17]

[14]Nellas, *Deification in Christ*, 37.
[15]Nellas, *Deification in Christ*, 39.
[16]Nellas, *Deification in Christ*, 41.
[17]Nellas, *Deification in Christ*, 41f.

Having set out the background in this way, Nellas now tackles the question of the nature of the "garments of skin." The notion of the empirical world as less than fully natural is, says Nellas, central to "the teaching of the Fathers on human nature," which "forms, as it were, a bridge with two piers." The first pier, he continues, is "the understanding of what is 'in the image'." The second is "the deeply significant notion of 'garments of skin'." These garments of skin are to be interpreted partly in terms of what is necessary for survival in man's postlapsarian state, but also partly in terms of the need to foster in a more positive way "his return to what is 'in the image.'"[18]

Intrinsic to the notion of the garments of skin, says Nellas, is the notion of mortality. The fall, he says, though in one sense a fall into materiality, is not to be identified simply with a fall into created matter. According to St Gregory of Nyssa, for example, although the body has become "coarse and solid" through the fall, and is characterized by a "gross and heavy composition," it will, at the general resurrection, recover its prelapsarian state, being "respun" into "something lighter and more aerial." The body will not be left behind, as a Gnostic dualism might maintain, but will be transfigured into its original beauty. Moreover, Nellas notes, it is not only the body that is, for St Gregory, in need of this transformation. He insists that the functions of the soul must also undergo a transformation, having become "corporeal" through the fall.[19] Thus, while St Gregory, more than most patristic writers, may seem to identify the garments of skin with the postlapsarian human body, he is, according to Nellas, actually "referring to the entire postlapsarian psychosomatic clothing of the human person."[20]

[18]Nellas, *Deification in Christ*, 44.
[19]Nellas, *Deification in Christ*, 5of.
[20]Nellas, *Deification in Christ*, 50 n. 92.

It is in the work of St Maximos the Confessor that Nellas sees the implications of this view being most fully worked out. Despite the fact that Maximos' work is "so dense and so rich in different layers of meaning" that Nellas feels his own interpretation of it to be somewhat provisional,[21] he feels confident in seeing as central to it the biblical statement that it was God who gave the garments of skin to humanity (Gen 3.21). This, says Nellas, is interpreted by Maximos in terms of the way in which "God acts in a loving way even to those who have become evil, so as to bring about our correction."[22]

The point here, says Nellas, is that although at one level the garments of skin are an evil, brought about as a direct result of human rebellion against the divine intention, God "changes that which is the result of denial and is therefore negative into something relatively positive." The garments of skin are therefore, he goes on, "a second blessing to a self-exiled humanity." God has added this blessing "like a second nature to the existing human nature, so that by using it correctly humanity can survive and realize its original goal in Christ."[23]

Moreover, says Nellas, it is not only such obvious evils as death that can be seen in this way. Following St John Chrysostom, he relates the garments of skin to human work, to the arts and sciences, and to politics. In these aspects of human life, he says, we can see particularly clearly how the garments of skin "are not unrelated to the iconic faculties of man before the fall." God, he goes on, has enabled "the attributes of that which is 'in the image'—the attributes which were transformed into 'garments of skin' without being changed in essence—to be useful to man not

[21]Nellas, *Deification in Christ*, 59.
[22]Nellas, *Deification in Christ*, 60, quoting St Maximos the Confessor, *Scholia on the Divine Names* 4.33 (PG 4:305D).
[23]Nellas, *Deification in Christ*, 61.

only in his struggle for mere survival but also as a means of making the new journey towards God."[24]

An aspect of the garments of skin that Nellas also discusses is their relationship to the more general cosmic ramifications of the fall. The laws that govern that order, while they continue to operate after the fall, are seen as doing so in a way that allows what the West calls "natural" evil—that is, they operate "in a disorganized and disordered way, and they involve man too in this disordered operation with the result that they draw him into misery and anguish."[25] These cosmic implications of the fall have, however, also been transformed by God. Like the human garments of skin, they constitute not only a penalty but also a remedy.[26]

Because of this kind of understanding, patristic writers usually express themselves in a way that manages, ultimately, not only to preserve the notion of the goodness of the created world, but also to point to the way in which the problems inherent in some of its aspects may be resolved. The world as we experience it is, for this approach, one that is appropriate to our fallen state, not only because its relative opaqueness to God's will reflects that state, but also because it remains sufficiently transparent to the divine intention to lead us towards the "new creation."

For an Orthodox theology that seeks to be sensitive to modern science, an important question arises at this point: that of whether this vision—of a cosmos with a "fallen" character that has its origins in human rebellion against God—can still be accepted. At one level, it clearly has its attractions since, as we have seen, it can supplement in a subtle and powerful way the kind of perspective on the problem of natural evil that has been developed by Western Christians in a more purely philosophical manner. At

[24]Nellas, *Deification in Christ*, 90f.

[25]Nellas, *Deification in Christ*, 62.

[26]Nellas, *Deification in Christ*, 63 n. 128, drawing attention to Chrysostom's *On Greeting Priscilla* 3.5 (PG 51:194).

another level, however, a major question arises: that of whether we can really give any significant weight to an understanding that is apparently tied so inextricably to a notion of the fall as a *historical* event. This notion of a fall within cosmic history is clearly incompatible with our scientific understanding of the world because it is evident, if we accept that understanding, that evil did not enter the world only after some historical event in which humans rebelled against God. Death, for example, clearly existed long before the evolutionary emergence of humans, as did painful diseases of the kind that are sometimes evident in the fossil remains of dinosaurs.

Before we conclude that the traditional understanding of the fall must be abandoned, however, we must ask precisely what it was that was at the heart of that understanding. Here, it is important to recognize Orthodox thinking about this issue has not always seen the "sequence" set out in Genesis—of creation, fall, and "this world"—in simple historical terms. Interesting questions about the traditional understanding of the fall and its cosmic effects have, for example, been posed in recent years by Orthodox scholars such as Christos Yannaras[27] and Paul Ladouceur,[28] while even in the patristic era similar questions seem to have arisen from Origen's speculation.

One example of this aspect of patristic thinking is related to the way in which, as we have seen, some of the Fathers believed, with St Gregory of Nyssa, that our present body has become "coarse and solid" through the fall but will, at the general resurrection, recover its prelapsarian state, being "respun" into "something lighter and more aerial."[29] This was understood, according to Nel-

[27]Christos Yannaras, *The Enigma of Evil* (Brookline, MA: Holy Cross Orthodox Press, 2012).

[28]Paul Ladouceur, "Evolution and Genesis 2–3: The Decline and Fall of Adam and Eve," *St Vladimir's Theological Quarterly* 57 (2013): 135–176.

las, in terms of the way in which our existence in the Paradisal state should not be identified with our current biological makeup, which is an aspect of the "garments of skin" given to us by God. Rather, as he puts it, God, by "allowing man to dress himself in biological life, the fruit of sin . . . redirected death, which was also the fruit of sin, against biological life, and thus by death is put to death not man but the corruption which clothes him."[30] In a related way, the fall was often seen, in the patristic era, as being not only a transition into our present biological state, but also into time as we now experience it. As Philip Sherrard has put it, it was a lapse "*into* a materialized space-time universe."[31]

In this perspective, the expulsion from Paradise involved much more of a discontinuity than is often appreciated, since not only was our "original" life not biological life, it was, in addition, not even a temporal existence in the usual sense of that term. (This notion can be explored and expanded, it should be noted, in terms of St Maximos the Confessor's notion of the simultaneity of creation and fall, in which, as one modern scholar has put it, "any actual, prelapsarian existence is purely hypothetical."[32])

---

[29]This relates to an aspect of the Origenist tradition that influenced many of the Fathers, who stressed *to noeron*—the soul's intellectual state or intellectual nature. Rational beings were, in this Origenist perspective, seen as having been created as a unique "intellectual substance" which was later broken up by the fall into individualized portions, each endowed with a "heavy body." While aspects of Origenism were later seem as heretical, this concept often remained in Orthodox thinking. (For Athanasius, for example, "virtue consists of the soul preserving its intellectuality [*to noeron*] according to nature.") For a discussion and references, see Norman Russell, "Bishops and Charismatics in Early Christian Egypt," in Behr, Louth, and Conomos, *Abba: The Tradition of Orthodoxy in the West*, 99ff.

[30]Nellas, *Deification in Christ*, 64.

[31]Sherrard, *Christianity and Eros*, 26 (my italics).

[32]Adam G. Cooper, *The Body in St Maximus the Confessor: Holy Flesh, Wholly Deified* (Oxford: Oxford University Press, 2005), 80.

This kind of understanding of the the character of our unfallen state has been explored by modern Orthodox scholars like Fr Sergius Bulgakov, who have suggested that the fall should be seen, not as a historical event, but as a "meta-historical" one.[33] This may be a somewhat difficult concept to understand, but just as Nellas himself, as we have seen, speaks in another context of "the supra-temporal reality of God,"[34] so also it may be necessary to talk about the "pre"-lapsarian state of humanity in comparable supra-temporal terms.

This notion of meta-historicity does not, it should be noted, mean that we have to abandon altogether the notion of a fall within the ordinary temporal process, since clearly the supra-temporal fall envisaged in this strand of Orthodox thought may be seen as reflected and manifested in the emergence of a knowledge of the ambiguity of self-centered behavior in our early ancestors. From a purely scientific perspective, this emergence was clearly a feature of some stage in our evolution. We may not be able to say precisely when the first human decision was made, within our space-time universe, to "rebel against God" and thus to manifest within time a "supra-temporal" attitude already meta-historically chosen. Nevertheless, we cannot avoid accepting that such a decision must, at some point in time, actually have been made. Thus, even if we feel the need to speak of a gradual emergence of a moral sense, and of "Adam's" decision to rebel against God as being constituted in history by many individual decisions, we can still affirm the historical basis of the Genesis story provided that we see the cosmic "consequences" of this rebellion as occurring before its historical manifestation. This is possible if we can see this historical manifestation as having been, in some sense, "anticipated" by God in his ordering of the creation.

[33]Sergius Bulgakov, *The Bride of the Lamb* (Grand Rapids: Wm. B. Eerdmans Publishing, 2002), 164ff.

[34]Nellas, *Deification in Christ,* 35.

In the light of all this, it may perhaps be too much of a generalization to say—as Robin Amis does—that when early Christian thinkers write of the fall, "they write of it not as a historical event but a 'psychological event'."[35] Amis's comment does, nevertheless, point us towards an important component of patristic thought, and this component is one that clearly challenges any claim that the notion of the fall has become redundant because of science.

But the precise details of how we should understand the fall in the light of science are irrelevant to the main point that we need to note here. This is that the general notion of the fall that has been developed within Orthodoxy points accurately to central aspects of our existential experience. The situation of frustration, meaninglessness, and evil in which we often find ourselves is one that truly exists, and it is from this situation that God has, according to Christian belief, undertaken to rescue us in and through Christ.

In this sense our present situation—however we think it came about—is not a "natural" one at all, if we use that term as the Orthodox Tradition tends to—i.e., in relation to God's original and ultimate intentions. The notions of the "subnatural" state of our present universe and of the garments of skin are, therefore, not ones that are irrelevant to us, even if we have reservations about the particular way in which they were originally formulated or are sometimes now understood. Whatever our reservations may be, these notions still provide a subtle and illuminating perspective on God's intentions—intentions which are, according to Christian belief, to be fully manifested in the "world to come," but which are frustrated in "this world" by our fallen state. Ours is not the truly natural world that God saw as "good" at the time of its creation, but a distorted version of that world, albeit with grace still perceptible in its modes of operation.

[35]Robin Amis, *A Different Christianity: Early Christian Esotericism and Modern Thought* (Albany: State University of New York, 1985), 48.

This understanding is highly relevant to the question of how we may speak of God acting in a world characterized by obedience to "laws of nature." For the Orthodox Tradition, while sometimes speaking about God acting in a way that is "above" nature, has tended, as we have seen, to avoid the technical distinction between the natural and the supernatural used in the West. Rather, because of the Orthodox view that there is "no natural or normal state, since grace is implied in the act of creation itself,"[36] Orthodox theologians have tended to think about divine action in a far more subtle (if usually less systematic) way than has been characteristic of Western writers.

This may be illustrated by the question of how God acts in and through the sacraments (or, as we Orthodox tend to call them, the "mysteries") of the Church. For Orthodox scholars, a sacrament is not only, as for their Western counterparts, an outward and visible sign of an inward and spiritual grace; it is also something more: what Fr Alexander Schmemann calls "a revelation of the genuine *nature* of creation."[37] Philip Sherrard, in particular, has stressed this aspect of the Eastern patristic understanding, noting that a sacrament is not "something set over against, or existing outside, the rest of life . . . something extrinsic, and fixed in its extrinsicality, as if by some sort of magical operation or *Deus ex machina* the sacramental object is suddenly turned into something other than itself." On the contrary, he goes on, "what is indicated or revealed in the sacrament is something universal, the intrinsic sanctity and spirituality of all things, what one might call their real nature."[38]

[36]Lossky, *Mystical Theology*, 101.

[37]Alexander Schmemann, *The Eucharist: Sacrament of the Kingdom* (Crestwood, NY: St Vladimir's Seminary Press, 1987), 33f.

[38]Philip Sherrard, "The Sacrament," in A. J. Philippou, ed., *The Orthodox Ethos: Essays in Honour of the Centenary of the Greek Orthodox Archdiocese of North and South America* (Oxford: Holywell Press, 1964), 1:134.

What makes the sacrament necessary, Sherrard goes on to explain, is simply the way in which the fall has led to the created order's "estrangement and alienation from its intrinsic nature." In the sacrament, he says, "this divided, estranged and alienated state is transcended," and the created order's "essential and intrinsic nature is revealed."[39] This means, he continues, that the sacrament is "reality itself, as it is in its naked essence and without anything being changed or symbolized or substituted." Because of this, he says, terms such as "transubstantiation" or "transformation" are ones which "tend to lead to confusion," since at the deepest level "nothing need be transubstantiated or transformed." The sacrament is a transformation only insofar as it is "a re-creation of the world 'as it was in the beginning.'"[40] In this understanding, a sacrament is simply a manifestation of the true reality of some aspect of this world, so that its usual relative opaqueness to God's purposes for it, and presence within it, gives way to a complete transparency.

This notion of the potential for any part of the created order to become more fully transparent to the purposes and presence of God is an extremely important one when we come to consider God's action in more general terms. For while the created order evidently has a certain transparency to the purposes of God before any specific human invocation of divine grace, it is clearly not fully transparent to those purposes prior to that invocation. The way in which the universe has evolved naturalistically does, certainly, already indicate some degree of transparency to the divine purpose, as does the fact that its beauty and awesomeness can lead us directly to praise God as its Creator. As the problem of natural evil indicates, however, this transparency is only relative. In a "fallen" world there is also a degree of opaqueness to

[39]Sherrard, "The Sacrament," 135.
[40]Sherrard, "The Sacrament," 139.

God's purposes. Nevertheless—as the centrality of intercessory prayer to the Christian tradition indicates—this opaqueness may be overcome, and what western Christians call God's "special" providence can be brought about, through the human recognition and invocation of God's will.

From this perspective, divine action in the world may be illuminated by the nature of the sacramental mysteries in a profound way. Quite simply, the events that Western theologians have usually spoken of in terms of God's "special" action may be seen, not as the product of some kind of divine interference with the world, in which the laws of nature are set aside or manipulated. Rather, they may be seen as the outward manifestation in this world of something that is already present but hidden within it: what we can properly call its "natural" state. The miraculous is not, in this perspective, the result of something being added to the world. It is, rather, the wiping away from that world of the grime of its fallen state, in order to reveal it in its pristine splendor.

Thus, in this perspective, while the old Western distinction between "general" and "special" modes of divine action is rendered superfluous, at another level the distinction remains meaningful. Its meaning lies, however, not in the traditional Western distinction between modes of divine action, but in a distinction between different degrees of human response to the divine will. "General" divine action corresponds to those aspects of the world that are, independently of the human response to God, still sufficiently transparent for God's purposes to be fulfilled. These will include all those naturalistic and scientifically explorable processes that have allowed the evolutionary emergence of beings who can respond to God in faith. "Special" divine action may be seen as corresponding to those "natural" aspects of the world that are, so to speak, present but inoperative until that response is made.

In this perspective, when the universe "changes" so as to bring about events of "special" providence, it is a sign and a foretaste of what is "naturally" to be when all the purposes of God have been fulfilled. In such an event, created things are, in the deepest sense, simply becoming themselves as they are in the intention of God. As the grime of fallen human nature gets wiped away in any person through response to God in faith, not only is the fullness of human potential that is revealed to us in Jesus Christ actualized in that person to some degree, but in addition, the world around that person may also be cleansed, and become "natural" once more. In this perspective, "special" divine providence is inextricably linked to human sanctity, so that it is, for example, no accident that anticipatory experiences of the wolf dwelling with the lamb (cf. Is 11.6) are linked in the memory of the Christian community to the response of wild animals to people like St Cuthbert of Lindisfarne and St Seraphim of Sarov.

It is in this way that we can see the appropriateness of speaking of miracles. They are not, for this perspective, the result of supernatural interventions in which the laws of nature are set aside, nor are they manipulations of those laws "from outside." They are, rather, what we might call manifestations of "higher laws of nature" which reflect—more fully than those which are scientifically explorable—God's presence in all things. It is of considerable interest, in this context, that when St Augustine of Hippo spoke about miracles, he did so, as we shall see presently, in comparable terms.

This view may not represent any standard exposition of the Orthodox Tradition, which hitherto has not had to speak about divine action in the kind of abstract way that has been usual in the West. Echoes of it are to be found, nevertheless, in the writings of many Orthodox scholars, and it is arguable that because of issues arising from the sciences, Orthodoxy does now need to articulate its instincts about these issues more clearly. In particular, as we shall see, it must not only challenge the pretensions to completeness of the kind of naturalism that relates only to the sub-natural world of ordinary experience; it must, in addition, explore the possibility of seeing all divine action in terms of an "enhanced naturalism" that reflects the realities of the "truly natural" world that we shall experience fully only in the world to come.

chapter twelve

NATURALISM AND
THE MIRACULOUS

The Orthodox notion that the miraculous reflects the "natural" character of the cosmos—as opposed to the "sub-natural" character of our present, fallen universe—poses the question of how we are to understand the relationship between these different states of the cosmos. On the one hand, our Orthodox belief in miraculous events points to discontinuity, since in the "subnatural" world these events are a rarity rather than the norm. On the other hand, patristic perspectives point to a kind of continuity. The "garments of skin" that are characteristic of the fallen world are not, as Panayiotis Nellas notes, "unrelated to the iconic faculties of man before the fall." God, he goes on, has enabled "the attributes of that which is 'in the image'—the attributes which were transformed into 'garments of skin' without being changed in essence—to be useful to man not only in his struggle for mere survival but also as a means of making the new journey towards God."[1]

This combination of continuity and discontinuity may, I have argued, be understood philosophically by interpreting the naturalism of the scientist as only as an aspect of what I have called the "enhanced naturalism" that is characteristic of the world to

[1]Nellas, *Deification in Christ*, 90f.

come. At a philosophical level, I have not explored this enhanced naturalism—at least initially—in terms of the *miraculous* as such, because this term is usually misunderstood in terms of a particular notion of the supernatural. Rather, I have focused on the more neutral concept of the *paranormal*, since important philosophical questions arise from the fact that repeatable experimental demonstration of paranormal phenomena—telepathy, telekinesis and the like—has proved impossible despite more than a century of research by scientists associated with bodies like the Society for Psychical Research.[2]

The philosophical question that I have considered is that of how events that excite wonder, because of their rarity and inexplicable nature, should be understood in terms of our present understanding of a cosmos that obeys "laws of nature." Are these events to be understood as violations of these laws, as many defenders of the miraculous usually assume? Or should we understand them in a more subtle way? As we have already noted, the eighteenth century philosopher, David Hume, argued that recognition that we live in a cosmos characterized by obedience to such laws makes it impossible for us to believe in miracles. As we shall see, however, this argument is flawed in a number of ways.

If we ask why most scientists do not accept that paranormal events occur, a major factor is their stress on the the importance of *repeatability* for the scientific methodology. To be accepted as scientific evidence, what is observed by one researcher in

[2]The Society for Psychical Research, founded in the United Kingdom in 1882, had many reputable academics as members during its early decades—including many abroad—who supported its aims of investigating paranormal phenomena through scientific methods. The center of gravity of such research moved to the US in the 1930s, especially through the establishment of J. B. Rhine's parapsychology laboratory at Duke University. But (as discussed below) it now has far fewer reputable scientists interested in its activities.

one laboratory or observatory must be observable by another researcher in another laboratory or observatory. Reported phenomena that are not susceptible to this repeatability criterion are rightly ignored as *scientific* evidence. The question remains, however, of whether rational agents should entirely ignore anecdotal evidence of paranormal events simply because this repeatability criterion is apparently violated.

An important point to note here is that the very notion of causality is one that requires more careful philosophical consideration than it is often given. An example sometimes cited in philosophical discussion of this topic is that of how we might think about the cause of a forest fire. Most of us, faced with this question, might speculate about possible causes in terms of an event like a lightning strike or a carelessly discarded match. But some philosophers have pointed out the inadequacy of such an answer by comparing it with the answer that might be given by the hypothetical passengers in a Venusian spaceship flying overhead. Their reaction—as beings from a world with an atmosphere very different from our own—would quite possibly be something like, "What can you expect when the Earth's atmosphere has so much oxygen in it?"

The point of this parable is that a full explanation of any event in terms of natural causality requires knowledge of the total context in which that event occurs, and aspects of this context are easily ignored and may even be unknown.[3] In the case of a forest fire, not only is the composition of the earth's atmosphere an important contributory factor, but so also is the fact that the woody material available in a forest reacts to heat input and to the presence of abundant oxygen by giving out much more heat than

[3]This would have been the case with scientists of the early modern period faced with a forest fire, since at that time they had no notion of the existence of oxygen.

was put in. (This is by no means the case in all chemical reactions.) A full explanation of the forest fire requires far more than simply identifying some event that provided an initial heat input.

Over and above this kind of issue, there is also a broader issue of complexity, which we have already examined in considering the concept of emergence. What is possible in the laboratory or observatory relies on screening out factors that may interfere with, or mask, the effects that are sought. But because of the complexity of the real world, this screening is often difficult.[4] Indeed, the greater the complexity of the situation, the harder it is to separate out different effects, and moreover—as we noted in our discussion of emergence—sometimes quite new and unexpected properties of complex wholes arise from holistic effects.

Some of the issues that arise from such considerations are evident from the present confused status of scientific research into paranormal phenomena. Important questions, as we have noted, arise from the fact that repeatable experimental demonstration of such phenomena has proved impossible despite more than a century of research. Many scientists, in the face of these negative results, now simply dismiss the possibility of such phenomena, putting all anecdotal evidence of their occurrence down to fraud, wishful thinking, or pure coincidence. (Indeed, paranormal research is now far less reputable in the scientific community than it was a century ago.[5]) Others, however, consider that the strength

[4]For example, some decades ago, the compilers of a catalogue of astronomical sources detectable at radio frequencies found, to their great embarrassment, that some of the "astronomical objects" they confidently listed were due to spurious signals caused by local electric fences.

[5]Although there is still some involvement in the Society for Psychical Research by some scientists, very few "great" names are now associated with it. Indeed, by contrast with the situation in the Society's early days, it would be thought by many within the scientific community that it would be disastrous for the progression of any young scientist's career to take more than a passing interest in such things. The continuing involvement of one

of at least some of this anecdotal evidence is such as to suggest that phenomena of this sort do occur, despite their being extremely difficult (and perhaps impossible) to investigate through experimental methods. After all, they say, people continue to fall in love with one another despite the fact that this process has never been observed under laboratory conditions. Might there not, they ask, be some strongly "personal" element at work in paranormal phenomena that similarly inhibits such observation?

If we take the view that paranormal events do occur, then how are we to understand them? Are we to think of them as examples of the laws of nature being violated, or should be think of them in some other way? Much depends on how we understand the concept of laws of nature. Some, for example, will assume that the laws of nature are always in principle susceptible to scientific investigation. Other than in terms of violation of those laws, therefore, they will be unable to conceptualize events that are reported but seem not to be susceptible to scientific investigation. Others may assume that laws of nature will always correspond to a "common sense" understanding of the kinds of thing that are possible. These will, once again, conceptualize paranormal events as necessarily being violations of these laws (and thus will tend to deny that they occur). But, as we have seen, the effects of holistic factors and of emergent complexity may make the first of these assumptions invalid, while physicists in particular will realize that reliance on a "common sense" criterion is very questionable. (This is perhaps the reason that they less often seem to be strident atheists than biologists are.) Not only do relativity and quantum mechanics notoriously defy "common sense," but physicists are also aware of historical examples of unpredicted phenomena that

"great name"—Brian Josephson—is arguably tolerated within the scientific community only because of the quality of his Nobel-prize-winning work on more conventional scientific topics.

at the time of their first observation seemed impossible in terms of then-current understanding.

The simplest example of this is perhaps the phenomenon of the complete disappearance of electrical resistance in certain materials when they are cooled to below a certain threshold temperature, so that an electric current persists indefinitely in a circuit without any applied power source. Discovered in 1911, this *superconductivity* was soon accepted as a scientifically-explorable phenomenon because of its repeatability, but it resisted adequate theoretical explanation for several decades. This unambiguously naturalistic phenomenon provides an example of what scientists sometimes call *regime change*, in which there is a discontinuity in physical properties when certain conditions are met—in this case, the properties of certain materials and very low temperature. It is not that the laws of nature have changed or been violated, but rather that, in certain circumstances, potential effects that are "normally" inoperative become significant.

It has sometimes been suggested by Western Christian commentators, including John Polkinghorne, that regime change of this kind provides a possible analogy for our thinking about miracles.[6] (Indeed, one of them, Robert John Russell, has gone as far as to see Christ's resurrection as "the first instantiation of a new law of nature."[7]) Is this, we must ask, a possible way forward for us in thinking about miracles? Such a way of speaking does, admittedly, seem at first sight to undermine the role of God in miraculous happenings, but three things should prevent us from assuming that this must necessarily be the case.

[6]See, e.g., John Polkinghorne, *One World: The Interaction of Science and Theology* (London: SPCK, 1986), 74ff.

[7]Robert John Russell, "Bodily Resurrection, Eschatology, and Scientific Cosmology," in Ted Peters, Robert John Russell, and Michael Welker, eds., *Resurrection: Theological and Scientific Assessments* (Grand Rapids: Eerdmans, 2002), 3ff.

First, Orthodoxy stresses that God is present and active in all natural processes. What happens through those processes is therefore not—as it would be within a deistic understanding—something with which God is not directly involved. Second, there is a sense in which, for any Christian understanding, all God's actions are susceptible in principle to the kind of understanding that lies behind our thinking about laws of nature. Christians assume God's *consistency*, so that if certain circumstances are found, then certain consequences may be expected to follow. If, in what seem to us to be identical situations, it happens that different effects result from divine action, we tend to assume, not that God is being capricious, but that we are wrong in our belief that the situations were identical.

The third thing that we need need to consider is, however, perhaps the most important for Orthodox. This is that something similar to this regime change analogy was occasionally hinted at by the Fathers of the church. In particular, in the work of St Augustine of Hippo, there is a clear implication that highly unusual events are able to occur because—over and above the kind of natural laws that we are able to understand—there is a "higher" law-like framework that the cosmos also obeys, which is in practice beyond human understanding. If there are simple systems that are susceptible to our understanding in terms of the "lower" law, this is only, Augustine seems to suggest, because the threshold has not been reached at which the influences of this "higher" component of the way the cosmos operates become operative.[8]

Augustine is, it must be admitted, a figure who is often regarded with ambivalence by Orthodox scholars, and in certain respects

---

[8]St Augustine, *Of the Advantages of Believing* 34, cf. *City of God* 21.6–8; see the comments in Wolfhart Pannenberg, "The Concept of Miracle," *Zygon: Journal of Religion and Science* 37 (2002): 759–762.

understandably so.[9] Here, however, while expressing himself in a way that was not characteristic of the Eastern patristic tradition, he was echoing something important in that tradition. This is the way in which, as we have noted, God must be seen as at work in his creation, not as an outside agent who interferes from time to time, but as the animating fire at the heart of all created things, responsible for all events, whether they are perceived as being natural or "above nature."

If we pursue this "higher law" analogy, however, we do need to be able to distinguish what, in paranormal events, is directly in accord with the will of God and what arises more indirectly through being "permitted"—even when used for purposes other than God's. (We can, after all, use the "lower" laws of nature for good or ill, and those described as black magicians claim—whether with justification or not—to have the ability to manipulate paranormal forces for purposes other than God's.)

An important point here is the way in which the Fourth Gospel speaks of the miraculous events that it reports as "signs" (*sēmeia.*) These, as biblical commentators have long recognized, have an explicitly theological function in that Gospel, in terms of conveying spiritual insight, the nature of which is indicated in the Gospel by the discourses with which the "sign" passages are interwoven in the text. In general, we can perhaps express this function of the "sign" in terms of an existential deepening of understanding and commitment.[10]

[9]Much of what Orthodox see as a distortion of Christian theology in the West arises from "Augustinian" perspectives. We should be aware, however, that some of these perspectives—albeit with roots in St Augustine's writings—may perhaps be the result, not of those writings themselves, but of the way in which later "Augustinians" tried to systematize them. Nevertheless, as we have noted, Augustine's understanding of the fall did certainly cause what was, from an Orthodox perspective, a major blind-spot in much Western Christian writing.

[10]One Western writer, the Anglican bishop, Ian Ramsey, has spoken

understood for paranormal events either to be denied as impossible or to be understood in any one particular way.

At this stage of our exploration, an important point can be made. We have already noted that the term *supernatural*—with its implication that the laws of nature have been set aside in favor of some direct action of God—may not be a good translation of the patristic notion of events that are *above nature*. In this chapter, we have looked at the modern concept of the *paranormal*, and we can see that it is arguable that although patristic usage is not entirely uniform, it often has more in common with the notion of the *paranormal* than it has with the term *supernatural* as it is often understood in the West. For, as we have noted, when something occurs that is seen by the Fathers as above nature, the term *nature* is being used to describe nature as we usually experience it. Yet some of the Fathers also speak, as we have seen, about the *true* nature of the cosmos as originally created and envisaged by God, which is to be restored when that cosmos attains its eschatological state. It is the relationship between these two "natures" that is at the heart of the patristic understanding of the miraculous, and it is arguable that the kind of "enhanced naturalism" that we have begun to explore in this chapter and the last provides a way of interpreting this relationship. Indeed, as we shall see in the next chapter, when this enhanced naturalism is explored in terms of the Orthodox doctrine of creation, it becomes not an abstract philosophical notion but something with far more depth: an *incarnational naturalism* in which the miraculous becomes fully integrated into our theological understanding of the cosmos.

chapter thirteen

INCARNATIONAL
NATURALISM

O ne of the results of the scientific revolution in the early
modern era was an increasing stress on the functioning
of the world according to "laws of nature." Because
of the new science, phenomena that had previously been attributed to God's direct action increasingly became understandable
in terms of these laws, and some began to wonder whether eventually all events would come to be understood in this way. Eighteenth-century philosophers sometimes went further and argued
that, to all intents and purposes, this understanding was in fact
already substantiated, so that the notion of miracles—with the
possible exception of the act of creation itself—had become redundant. Among those who accepted this view were the deists, who
accepted the validity of arguments from design and so did not
become atheists. The god that they believed in was not, however,
the God of classical Christian belief, but simply a creator of the
cosmos who, after the moment of creation, had become nothing
more than what has been called an "absentee landlord."

At the heart of this Enlightenment-period discussion was a set
of assumptions that had at least some of their origins in medieval
Western thinking. Already, before the rise of scholasticism, there
had been a tendency to think about nature as something to which

divine grace was added as a supernatural gift. This tendency continued in scholasticism, in which, although God was still seen as the "primary" cause of all events, normal events were seen as also having a "secondary," natural cause. In the case of miracles, it was believed that there was no secondary cause, so that such events were seen as entirely supernatural.

This scholastic picture did have a certain subtlety, not only because God—as "primary" cause—was still seen as active in natural processes, but also because grace was always seen as "completing" nature. In the Enlightenment period, however, there was a tendency for this subtlety to be lost. The natural world was increasingly seen as a kind of clockwork mechanism understandable through science, and those who still believed in miracles tended to see God's continuing action in the world as limited to those events for which no scientific explanation could be found. There was thus a new emphasis on "gaps" in scientific explanation, and a view of God developed that is sometimes now referred to as the "God of the gaps."

In recent Western Christian discussion there has been a reaction against this model. This has led to a new stress on the way in which God should be seen as working *in, with, and under* the laws of nature. But, as we have noted, because Western Christian thinking has tended to assume a separation between God and the world, this stress inevitably poses the question of how "special" divine action can occur. If God is assumed to be "outside of" the world, then the question of how he can "get in" remains. This understanding of separation, with its emphasis on the autonomy of the cosmos' normal functioning, tends to see special divine action as requiring what is sometimes called a *causal joint* between God and the world, through which God can manipulate the outcome of those laws. Much effort has been expended in attempting to identify this causal joint in a way that is scientifically literate.

Typically, the non-determinism of the quantum mechanical picture of the world has provided the conceptual foundation for this effort. On the other hand, in an important study by Nicholas Saunders, the success of this model has been questioned.[1]

As an alternative to this approach I have—in my books, *Wrestling With the Divine*[2] and *The God of Nature*[3]—advocated an approach that is based both on philosophical arguments about the concept of naturalism and (particularly in the latter) on important aspects of Orthodox theology. In the philosophical component of this argument (as set out in the last chapter) I have argued that we need to take into account, not only miracles with a religious meaning, but all reported events of a paranormal kind. I have urged that—despite the difficulties of dealing with anecdotal evidence—we need not only to recognize the possibility of such events, but also to see them in a naturalistic way. This is possible, I have argued, by defining naturalism more broadly than it sometimes is: not in terms of what can in principle be uncovered by the scientific methodology, but in terms of the more general belief that the world always functions consistently—that is, in a way that we can describe in terms of obedience to "fixed instructions." These instructions, in their simpler manifestations, I see as susceptible to investigation through the scientific methodology, and thus nothing that represents robust scientific theory need, in

[1]Nicholas Saunders, *Divine Action and Modern Science* (Cambridge: Cambridge University Press, 2002). This model, which has set the terms of the debate about divine action within the so-called science-theology dialogue of the last half century, has been seen by Wesley Wildman as based on a "personalistic theism" that represents "a distinctively Protestant deviation from the mainstream Christian view." See Wesley Wildman, "Robert John Russell's Theology of God's Action," in Ted Peters and Nathan Hallanger, eds., *God's Action in the World: Essays in Honour of Robert John Russell* (Aldershot: Ashgate, 2006), 166.

[2]Christopher C. Knight, *Wrestling With the Divine.*

[3]Christopher C. Knight, *The God of Nature.*

my view, be challenged. But I argue that not all such instructions are necessarily susceptible to investigation through the scientific methodology, since at levels of high complexity—such as that of the *personal*—these fixed instructions will simply not be susceptible to the *repeatability* criterion that is so important for scientific methodology. (We cannot, for example, put two people in a laboratory and tell them to fall in love so that we can observe the process.) This is not to deny that such processes follow what we might call law-like patterns, with identical outcomes arising from identical situations. Rather, it means that there is an *epistemological* barrier to our exploration, in that the criteria for identifying identical situations are simply not available to us.

In terms of this understanding, I have suggested that naturalism need not, *a priori*, preclude events that are seen as paranormal or miraculous, since neither of these terms has any necessary connotations of the supernatural. (The root meaning of the term *miracle*, for example, is simply "that which excites wonder.") Such events, I have suggested, may be seen as coming within the bounds of an "enhanced" naturalism because they may be seen as analogous to what in physics are known as changes of regime, such as the onset of superconductivity in certain materials when they are cooled to below a particular temperature. In such changes, once a certain threshold is crossed, discontinuities in properties occur. The difference between this kind of regime change, which may be explored scientifically, and what is considered paranormal lies only, I have suggested, in the way in which, in the latter, the repeatability criterion is not straightforwardly applicable at a practical level, so that investigation through the scientific methodology becomes difficult or impossible.

It is at this point that patristic theological considerations come into play. The first of these considerations relates to an aspect of Western theological thinking in the period before that thinking became dominated by scholastic understandings. This is the way in which the philosophical distinction that I have made—between natural processes that are straightforwardly susceptible to scientific investigation and those that are not—may be understood in terms of the way in which St Augustine of Hippo, in the late fourth century, wrote about miracles. The point here is that we might now interpret his view as suggesting a distinction between "lower" and "higher" laws of nature. Miracles are not, in this approach "supernatural" events but instead are to be seen—in much the way that I have suggested—as outcomes of "higher" laws of nature that are not susceptible to our investigation.[4]

This understanding is, I believe, also supported by aspects of the Eastern patristic tradition. At the heart of my interpretation of this tradition is my observation that it rejects the separation between grace and nature that has influenced most Western theological systems (and that has its origins in aspects of the thinking of Augustine other than that to which I have already alluded). For Orthodoxy, there is—as Vladimir Lossky has noted—no concept "of 'pure nature' to which grace is added as a supernatural gift. For it, there is no natural or 'normal' state, since grace is implied by the act of creation itself."[5] This is linked to the way in which, as we have seen, the notion of the *supernatural* is not used in Orthodoxy in the same way as it is in the West.

The Orthodox view of the cosmos is, as we have also seen, one that is based on what is sometimes called panentheism: the notion that the world is not separated from God but is, in some sense, "in God." This panentheistic dimension of Orthodox understanding is not of the somewhat vague kind that has recently found a

---

[4]See St Augustine, *Of the Advantages of Believing* 34, cf. *City of God* 21:6–8; see also the comments in Pannenberg, "The Concept of Miracle," 759–762.

[5]Lossky, *Mystical Theology*, 101.

place in Western Christian thinking, but it has roots in important doctrinal understandings. It is perhaps manifested most clearly in the notion of divine energies in the work of St Gregory Palamas.[6] Certain aspects of Orthodox panentheism are, however, made clearer in the work of St Maximos the Confessor, who—in a way that reflects the range of meanings of the Greek term *logos*—speaks, not only about the divine *Logos* incarnate in Christ (Jn 1.1–14) but also about the *logos* of each created thing, which he sees as being, in some sense, a manifestation of the divine *Logos*. As Metropolitan Kallistos of Diokleia has put it, in Maximos' understanding, "Christ the creator Logos has implanted in every created thing a characteristic logos, a 'thought' or 'word,' which is God's intention for that thing, its inner essence which makes it distinctively itself and at the same time draws it towards the divine realm."[7]

An important point to note here is that Maximos' understanding of the *logoi* of created things includes—as Metropolitan Kallistos has noted—a sense of the way in which those things are, by their very nature, drawn towards their eschatological fulfilment. This insight, as I have observed in the books I have cited, seems to anticipate the kinds of teleological possibilities that in recent years have crept back into interpretations of scientific thinking, both through the notion of convergent evolution developed by Simon Conway Morris[8] and through some understandings of the astrophysicist's perception of the "fine tuning" of the universe.[9] Here, I have argued, we find a convergence between insights based on a naturalistic understanding and what I have called the

[6]Kallistos Ware, "God Immanent yet Transcendent," 157–168.

[7]Ware, "God Immanent yet Transcendent," 160.

[8]Simon Conway Morris, *Life's Solution*.

[9]Barrow and Tipler, *The Anthropic Cosmological Principle*, is now slightly outdated but still provides perhaps the best comprehensive review of the issues.

teleological-christological insights of St Maximos, for whom—as Vladimir Lossky has put it—the world, "created in order that it might be deified" is by its very nature "dynamic, tending always towards its final end." [10]

An understanding based on this convergence between naturalistic and theological perspectives may, I have argued, be analyzed in terms of Maximos' incarnational focus. It may be seen, I have suggested, as a kind of *incarnational naturalism*. This use of the term *naturalism* is reinforced for me by the way in which, as we have seen, another aspect of the Orthodox Tradition—its understanding of both sacraments and miracles—may also be interpreted in terms of a kind of naturalism. This is related to the Orthodox belief that the world has suffered a transformation in "the fall," and will undergo another transformation when its eschatological fulfilment is accomplished. In this sense, the world as we now experience it is seen in Orthodox theology as being far from what God originally intended and ultimately wills, so that in a sense it should be seen as "unnatural" or—perhaps better—sub-natural. The traditional Orthodox interpretation of the "garments of skin" given by God to humans after their rebellion against God (Gen 3.21) is that they represent our present, sub-natural, psychosomatic make-up, and that this make-up is reflected in the entire sub-natural world in which we find ourselves.[11] Miracles, for this understanding, are often at least implicitly seen in the same way as the sacraments explicitly are:[12] not as

---

[10]Lossky, *Mystical Theology*, 101.

[11]An aspect of this sub-natural character of the world is, as we have seen, that there exists within it what Western Christian analysis would call "natural evil."

[12]As we have noted, Alexander Schmemann calls the sacrament "a revelation of the genuine *nature* of creation," *The Eucharist*, 33f. In a comparable way, Philip Sherrard has also stressed this aspect of the Eastern patristic understanding, noting that a sacrament is not "something set over against,

"supernatural" events in the Western sense of that term, but as a restoration of the world's "natural" state—i.e., as an anticipation of its eschatological transformation, brought about through the faithful response of creatures to their Creator.[13]

The central argument of the books that I have cited is that the philosophical arguments that I have outlined may be combined with these essentially theological insights in a new synthesis. In this synthesis, the classic Western distinctions between special and general modes of divine action and between the natural and the supernatural are made redundant.

This argument has been seen by Sarah Lane Ritchie as an important component of what she calls a "theological turn"[14] in twenty-first century discussion of divine action. In relation to this theological turn, my own arguments, based on Orthodox insights, may be seen as anticipating aspects of more recent Western developments within that discussion. Ritchie has explored the way in which I—together with the Western proponents of this theological turn—reject the assumption on which most recent Western debate about divine action has been based: that of an

or existing outside, the rest of life . . . something extrinsic, and fixed in its extrinsicality, as if by some sort of magical operation or *Deus ex machina* the sacramental object is suddenly turned into something other than itself." On the contrary, he goes on, "what is indicated or revealed in the sacrament is something universal, the intrinsic sanctity and spirituality of all things, what one might call their real nature." See Philip Sherrard, "The Sacrament," 134–135.

[13]See Knight, *The God of Nature*, 86–95; cf. Christopher C. Knight, "The Fallen Cosmos: An Aspect of Eastern Christian Thought and its Relevance to the Dialogue Between Science and Theology," *Theology and Science* 6 (2008): 305–315.

[14]Sarah Lane Ritchie, "Dancing Around the Causal Joint: Challenging The Theological Turn in Divine Action Theories," *Zygon: Journal of Religion and Science* 37 (2017): 362–379. This paper has been expanded in an important book: Sarah Lane Ritchie, *Divine Action and the Human Mind* (Cambridge: Cambridge University Press, 2019).

essentially autonomous universe, which God must influence from the "outside." Those of us who challenge this kind of naturalism instead posit, in our various ways, a different kind of naturalism, based on a universe that is to be understood ultimately only in terms of God's presence within it. As Ritchie observes, we argue that standard Western understandings of divine action, of the causal joint kind, "are dependent upon question-begging metaphysical commitments, which in turn inadequately frame the entire divine action conversation. These presuppositions involve basic ontological questions about the God–nature relationship, and especially the question of what, exactly, it means to be properly 'natural.' "[15]

In relation to the concept of miracles, this "theological turn" manifests important parallels between my own approach, based on Orthodox insights, and that of a few Western Christian scholars involved in the "theological turn"[16]—especially those who emphasize the work of the Holy Spirit and have developed what Ritchie calls a "pneumatological naturalism." As we have seen, in my own way of expressing the Orthodox understanding, miraculous events are an aspect of the "natural" functioning of the world that normally requires human response to God to be activated. In a comparable way, the pneumatological approach is, as Ritchie puts it, one in which the way that "some events seem more supernatural than others . . . is due the varying levels of

[15]Ritchie, "Dancing Around the Causal Joint," 362.

[16]Ritchie sees two main components of the Western dimension of the "theological turn": the revision of scholastic assumptions in Michael Dodds, *Unlocking Divine Action: Contemporary Science and Thomas Aquinas* (Washington, DC: Catholic University of America Press, 2012), and the "pneumatological" versions to be found in Amos Yong, *The Spirit of Creation: Modern Science and Divine Action in the Pentecostal-Charismatic Imagination* (Grand Rapids: Eerdmans, 2011), and James A. K. Smith, *Thinking in Tongues: Pentecostal Contributions to Christian Philosophy* (Grand Rapids: Eerdmans, 2010).

creaturely response and openness to the Spirit."[17] Here she quotes James Smith as saying that such events are "sped-up modes of the Spirit's more regular presences,"[18] and this clearly parallels my own view of the way that such events may be seen as the outcome of the presence of the *Logos* in both "lower" and "higher" laws of nature.

Indeed, since Orthodox perspectives are always Trinitarian, the views of the Protestant pneumatologists are already implicitly present in Orthodox thinking about the presence of this *Logos*. (In the work of the Cappadocian Fathers, for example, divine action is always Trinitarian, and St Irenaeus sees the Son and the Spirit as the "two hands" of the Father.) What Ritchie's analysis of Western pneumatological thinking within the "theological turn" has made much clearer is that the Orthodox approach that I have presented—with its focus on the divine *Logos*—may be seen as only one aspect of the truly Trinitarian understanding that is intrinsic to Orthodoxy.

The reader of this book who wishes to explore further the "neo-Byzantine" model of divine action that I have discussed[19] must be referred to the books that I have cited, as well as to the book in which Ritchie analyzes the theological turn that she perceives in recent discussion of divine action.[20] As we have already seen in outline, however, this neo-Byzantine model is one in which

[17]Ritchie, "Dancing Around the Causal Joint," 375.

[18]James A. K. Smith, "Is the Universe Open for Surprise? Pentecostal Ontology and the Spirit of Naturalism," *Zygon: Journal of Religion and Science* 43 (2008): 892.

[19]This model was first presented in Christopher C. Knight, "Divine Action: A Neo-Byzantine Model."

[20]Ritchie, *Divine Action and the Human Mind*—in which the eighth chapter is devoted to what she calls my "panentheistic" model. This model is also discussed—albeit in a briefer way—in Neil Messer, *Science in Theology: Encounters Between Science and the Christian Tradition* (London: T and T Clark, 2020), 49–50.

the occurrence of miraculous events is not to be denied. Equally, however, these events are not to be understood in terms of the kind of naturalism that sees their occurrence as requiring God either to set aside the laws of nature or else to manipulate those laws through some kind of causal joint. In this model, an alternative to such approaches is to be found in a new and "enhanced" kind of naturalism—an *incarnational naturalism*—that is based on the way in which St Maximos the Confessor interprets the incarnation of the divine *Logos* in terms of the presence of that *Logos* in all created things.

Here, I have argued, the Augustinian notion of higher laws of nature provides a useful way of thinking about miraculous events, but it is supplemented in an important way when Orthodox insights are taken into account. For if the Augustinian notion is interpreted in terms of a picture of God and the creation as separated—as it usually is in the West—then it is in danger of falling into a deistic, "absentee landlord" understanding that is different from classical deism only insofar as it manages to avoid the deistic belief that miracles cannot occur. If, however, the notion of "higher laws of nature" is interpreted in terms of St Maximos' panentheistic picture, then any hint of the "absentee landlord" God of deism is removed because those events that we describe as miraculous are—like those that we can understand through science—ones from which God is not absent. In all events—whether understandable through science or otherwise—he can be seen as active and present.

What is envisaged here is not, it must be emphasized, an extension of the kind of classic deism in which God is envisaged as having, at some point in the past, created the world with certain "fixed instructions" built into it. Rather, as Ritchie has rightly noted in her analysis of the model I have articulated, the act of creation—incorporating the setting up of the fixed instructions—

is not, for this model, "to be thought of as occurring in the past; to do so is to presume an essentially erroneous relationship between God and time." One should not, she goes on, think of this setting up "as occurring in a far distant past—rather it is eternal and being subjectively experienced within temporal constraints."[21] It is in this way, she explains, that the model is not one in which we are unable to speak of God's personal responses to events in the world. Rather, the model is based on the argument that "responsiveness should not be conflated with temporality."[22]

This means, for example, that intercessory prayer is not, for this model, meaningless in the way that a deistic understanding would assume, nor are its results "impersonal" in the way that some would claim. As I have put it elsewhere, if a purely temporal perspective is adopted, then God is seen as knowing what we pray for only after we have prayed for it. Therefore, that prayer can be effective only if there is some mechanism by which God can "respond" to our prayer. But, I have observed, in terms of the classical view of divine eternity "this picture is simply rendered void. In this view, God does not have to 'wait' for our prayer to occur, but simply 'sees' it eternally. . . . It is not that God 'foresees' our prayer—although this concept can perhaps give us a hint of how God can be thought of as 'responding' to what has not yet happened. In terms of the classical model, God neither responds nor foresees in any literal sense of these terms. God simply acts and sees through a single linked action and vision."[23]

The advantages of this model are, I would argue, both theological and apologetic. At the theological level, the Orthodox doctrines of creation and incarnation are fully acknowledged by the model,

[21]Ritchie, *Divine Action and the Human Mind*, 286. The chapter of this book in which this remark is made—ch. 8—represents perhaps the best discussion of the model that has so far appeared.

[22]Ritchie, *Divine Action*, 282.

[23]Knight, *The God of Nature*, 131f.

while the common notion of supernatural intervention—which is based on an understanding of the cosmos that has non-Orthodox roots—is replaced by a more subtle understanding.

At the apologetic level, the widespread suspicion of the notion of "supernatural events" that is characteristic of our scientific age is acknowledged by this model as at least partially justified. In this sense, the model promises to do what was made possible in the early centuries by apologists such as St Justin Martyr and St Clement of Alexandria, who set out to convince their contemporaries that the Christian faith was compatible with important elements of the philosophy of their time. We do not—as some seem to think—have to challenge the naturalism that is almost instinctive among our contemporaries. Rather, we must interpret it theologically, expanding it in such a way that we can acknowledge both the validity of the scientific enterprise and the occurrence of those events that we call miraculous. The model that I have presented is able, I believe, to allow this interpretation to be made.

AFTERWORD

Throughout this book I have been critical of the way in which the Western science-theology dialogue has developed over the past half-century. Nevertheless, I believe that we need to be grateful to those involved in this development, because they have perceived the great apologetic need to explain how insights that arise from modern science may be seen as compatible with Christian belief, and have posed questions of the sort that we in the Orthodox community cannot ignore.

In our Orthodox community there will inevitably be some who are wary of my openness to this questioning. I can only respond to this wariness by saying that I believe that the questions that have been asked within the Western science-theology dialogue will inevitably occur in a scientific age. We cannot ignore those questions, nor can we ignore the answers that have been proposed by Western scholars, even when we judge them (as I do) to be inadequate or incomplete. They can, I believe, still be helpful to us in a way comparable to that indicated by Metropolitan Kallistos of Diokleia, when he says that "If we Orthodox are to fulfil our role properly, we must understand our own Tradition better than we have in the past, and it is the west . . . that can help us do this. We Orthodox must thank our younger brothers, for through contact with Christians of the west we are being enabled to acquire a new vision of Orthodoxy."[1]

[1]Ware, *The Orthodox Church*, 326.

In the same work, Metropolitan Kallistos makes the important point that loyalty to Tradition, "properly understood, is not something mechanical, a passive and automatic process of transmitting the accepted wisdom of an era in the distant past. . . . [Tradition] is constantly assuming new forms, which supplement the old without superseding them."[2]

Some of these new forms, as I have indicated, will arise from taking seriously Fr Georges Florovsky's insight into the way in which following the Fathers "does not mean simply to quote their sentences. It means to acquire their *mind*."[3] This insight, as we have seen, is related to the observation that in the patristic writings there is—mixed with the "wheat" of patristic insight—what Metropolitan Kallistos of Diokleia has described as the "chaff," which we must nowadays separate from the wheat if we are to be true to the patristic mind.[4]

This recognition is, I have argued, essential if we are to deal adequately with the way in which the Fathers often expressed their beliefs in terms of scientific understandings that were common in their own time but are now seen as inaccurate or even ludicrous. For those of us who recognize the need to separate this scientific chaff from the theological wheat of the Fathers' writings, their scientific inaccuracy does not affect the continuing accessibility of their religious meaning, since we can find ways of expressing that religious meaning that are not dependent on the precise way in which that meaning was originally expressed. It is this religious meaning that I have endeavored to retain and explicate in all that I have written in this book, attempting to ensure that what I have said is in accord with the way in which

[2]Ware, *The Orthodox Church*, 198.

[3]Georges Florovsky, "The Ethos of the Orthodox Church," *The Ecumenical Review* 12 (1960): 188.

[4]Ware, *The Orthodox Church*, 212.

Tradition can constantly assume new forms, "which supplement the old without superseding them."

The fear that some of my fellow-Orthodox may feel in the face of proposed supplements of this kind has been commented on in an interesting way by another metropolitan bishop of the our church. This is Metropolitan Anthony (Bloom) of Sourozh, who as a young man trained as a medical doctor, and later used the experience of science obtained in that training to explain his perceptions about such fears.

When a scientific model is first developed, says Metropolitan Anthony, a good scientist's reaction "will be to go round and round his model in all directions, examining and trying to find where the flaw is, what the problems are that are generated by the model he has built, by the theory he has proposed, by the hypothesis he has now offered for the consideration of others. . . . At the root of the scientist's activity is the certainty that what he is doubting is the model he has invented—that is, by the way he has projected his intellectual structures on the world around him and on the facts, the way in which his intelligence has grouped things. But what he is absolutely certain of is that the the reality that is beyond his model is in no danger if his model collapses. The reality is stable; it is there, the model is an inadequate expression of it, but the reality doesn't alter because the model shakes."[5] Because this distinction is fully understood in scientific work, says Metropolitan Anthony, the scientist's doubt "is hopeful, it is joyful, it is destructive of what he has done himself because he believes in the reality that is beyond and not in the model he has constructed." This, he goes on, is something "we must learn as believers for our spiritual life both in the highest forms of

[5]Metropolitan Anthony of Sourozh, *God and Man*, new ed. (Crestwood, NY: St Vladimir's Seminary Press, 1993), 51–52.

theology and in the small simple concrete experience of being a Christian."[6]

For Metropolitan Anthony, the spiritual and theological application of this insight is that God is the Reality, and that what we say about God is—as Orthodox apophaticism emphasizes—the model that we construct. If we know the Reality experientially, then we need have no fear about exploring the way in which concepts about that Reality may be open to new forms of expression. "Whenever we are confronted with a crossroads" says Metropolitan Anthony, "whenever we are in doubt, whenever our mind sees two alternatives, instead of saying 'Oh God make me blind, Oh God help me not to see, Oh God give me loyalty to what I now know to be untrue,' we should say 'God is casting a ray of light on something I have outgrown—the smallness of my original vision. I have come to the point where I can see more and deeper, thanks be to God'."[7]

I believe that we are now, through the sciences, truly in a position to develop our theological understanding in a way that enables us to see "more and deeper" than we sometimes have in the past. My hope and prayer is that what I have written here may be a contribution to that development, both for the theological scholars of our Orthodox community and for the ordinary believer.

[6]Metropolitan Anthony, *God and Man*, 51–52.
[7]Metropolitan Anthony, *God and Man*, 51–52.

INDEX